ALLYSA TOREY *and* **JENNIFER APPEL**

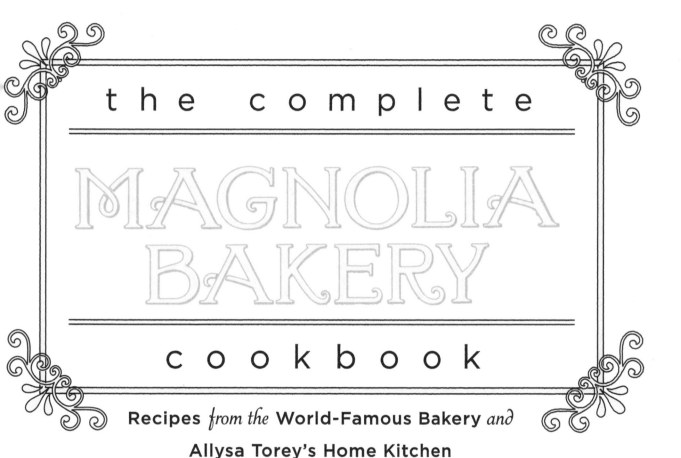

the complete

MAGNOLIA BAKERY

cookbook

Recipes *from the* **World-Famous Bakery** *and*

Allysa Torey's Home Kitchen

SIMON & SCHUSTER PAPERBACKS
New York London Toronto Sydney

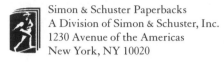
Simon & Schuster Paperbacks
A Division of Simon & Schuster, Inc.
1230 Avenue of the Americas
New York, NY 10020

This Simon & Schuster trade paperback edition November 2009

SIMON & SCHUSTER PAPERBACKS and colophon are registered trademarks of
Simon & Schuster, Inc.

For information about special discounts for bulk purchases,
please contact Simon & Schuster Special Sales at
1-866-506-1949 or business@simonandschuster.com.

The Simon & Schuster Speakers Bureau can bring authors to
your live event. For more information or to book an event,
contact the Simon & Schuster Speakers Bureau at
1-866-248-3049 or visit our website at www.simonspeakers.com.

Designed by Jaime Putorti

Manufactured in the United States of America

20 19 18 17 16 15 14

Library of Congress Cataloging-in-Publication Data

Torey, Allysa.
   The complete Magnolia Bakery cookbook : recipes from the world-famous bakery and
Allysa Torey's home kitchen / Allysa Torey and Jennifer Appel.
      p.   cm.
   Consists of the Magnolia Bakery cookbook / by Jennifer Appel and Allysa Torey and
More from Magnolia / by Allysa Torey.
   Includes index.
   1. Baking. 2. Desserts. 3. Magnolia Bakery. I. Appel, Jennifer. II. Appel, Jennifer.
Magnolia Bakery cookbook.   III. Torey, Allysa. At home with Magnolia.   IV. Title.
   TX765.T66   2009
   641.8'15—dc22   2009025903

ISBN 978-1-4391-7564-4

Acknowledgments

We would like to thank our agent, Carla Glasser, for creating this opportunity and the staff, past and present, at Simon & Schuster who helped put this book together.

We would also like to thank our families and friends for their endless support and for being such enthusiastic testers. Allysa would like to thank her former managing and baking staff at Magnolia for all of their hard work, and especially Margaret Hathaway for her contributions and assistance.

But mostly we would like to acknowledge and thank our wonderful customers, who continued to support us over the years despite the crazy long lines out the door.

Contents

CUPCAKES AND LAYER CAKES • 89

Introduction

When we first opened the Magnolia Bakery, we imagined a cozy, old-fashioned shop where people could come for a cup of coffee and something sweet. We expected our customers to include some local regulars and lots of neighborhood families. We thought we'd close at seven each evening so we could go home and make dinner. We never expected that Magnolia would turn into a city-wide hangout, much less that on weekend nights there would be lines out the door!

The Magnolia Bakery came into being over a brunch conversation during which Jennifer and I expressed for the umpteenth time our mutual frustration with our jobs and lifestyles. We finally decided that something would be done about it and opened up a wholesale baking business in early 1996. We soon received very positive feedback from our customers. When a retail space became available in our favorite neighborhood, we grabbed the opportunity. New York City's West Village seemed ideal. It was low-key and family-oriented, a place where we could do what we loved where we loved it. Over the course of two months and with the help of an adept construction crew, we transformed an empty shell into a warm cozy kitchen.

Our customers would stop by as much for the feel of the store as they did for the desserts. With its vintage American decor and desserts, customers often told us that walking into the bakery was just like stepping back in time to their grandmother's kitchen. They would come in for a slice of cake and end up with a little piece of their childhood. Over the years, people have wanted to meet us to say thanks for making the red velvet cake they remembered from church picnics or the banana pudding just like their mom used to make. While the business itself was fast paced and hectic at times, our original aim and values remained the same: we simply did everything the old-fashioned way, using the best and freshest ingredients, and took the time to produce delicious homemade treats.

A few years into business together, Jennifer left Magnolia to open up her own bakery, The Buttercup Bake Shop in midtown Manhattan. After the publication of *The Magnolia Bakery Cookbook*, many people suggested that I do a second book. While working full time at the bakery, the idea of writing another cookbook seemed impossible. Finally, after putting together a committed staff at the shop, I was able to move full time to my country house, and I could really consider the idea, knowing that I would have the time and energy necessary to write the book I wanted to write. I created the recipes for *More From Magnolia* in an old-fashioned style, but with new ideas and different combinations of ingredients to keep things interesting and fun.

As the unexpected popularity of our cupcakes grew, the bakery got busier and busier and the lines got longer and longer. After ten wonderful years at Magnolia, I decided to sell the business to stay home full time with my growing family. The new owners have opened more Magnolia Bakeries and continue to be successful.

This collection of recipes brings together all of the recipes in both Magnolia cookbooks—classic American desserts reflecting the sensibilities of the bakery and my home.

Allysa Torey

MAGNOLIA BAKERY

NEW YORK CITY

Helpful Hints

While we had to produce large quantities of desserts at Magnolia, we stuck to the philosophy of home baking and followed certain rules to make sure our product was tasty and of high quality every time. In this section, Allysa provides some suggestions to help you attain success as a home baker.

GENERAL BAKING HINTS

At the bakery, the best and freshest ingredients were always used, and a set procedure adhered to every time.

Before starting it is important to read through the recipe from beginning to end to ensure that you understand it thoroughly. Then assemble all the ingredients (to make sure you have everything!) and the necessary equipment you will need to make the process flow more smoothly.

The butter, eggs, and milk should be at room temperature before you even think about beginning a recipe. And if you're making a cheesecake, it is especially important that the cream cheese be at room temperature. Most of the recipes in this book and most cookbooks call for "softened" butter, but it is important to recognize that softened butter is actually butter at room temperature. If you press your finger into properly softened butter, it will leave an indentation but will retain its shape. If the butter is very soft, it is difficult to achieve the desired texture and density in baked goods. When making icing or frosting, let your butter get a bit softer than if you were baking a dessert. If the eggs need to be separated for your recipe, it's easier to separate them when they're cold and then allow them to come to room temperature.

When selecting the pans you will use, keep in mind that metal pans should be smooth, because uneven or blackened pans tend to absorb heat unevenly. For pies, brownies, and squares, glass baking dishes tend to work better than pans with a non-stick surface. You can grease the pans using a pastry brush or by rubbing in the butter or shortening with your fingers. Just make sure that, either way, the pan's surface is evenly and not overly coated. After greasing, sprinkle a few spoonfuls of flour into the pan, shake it around until the entire inside of the pan is coated with flour, and then empty out the excess flour by tapping the pan gently. When called for in the recipe, line the bottom of the pan with waxed paper. If you're making a cake, this is a foolproof way to prevent it from sticking to the pan.

CAKES

One of the most important tips concerns the creaming of butter. When creaming butter, it is necessary to beat the butter until it is light and fluffy, which takes about three minutes depending on the type of mixer you're using. Most people, especially if they're just learning to bake or if they don't bake very often, don't realize how long three minutes is, and so they wind up not creaming their butter for the proper amount of time. Creaming the butter properly ensures that the dessert (especially if it's a cake) will have the volume and texture desired. It is also important to add the sugar gradually, to beat continuously, and to keep beating for an additional two to three minutes. The eggs should then be added, one at a time, beating until the mixture is thick, fluffy, and pale in color. Up to this point it is almost impossible to beat the batter too much.

To make it easier to alternately add the ingredients, thoroughly combine (or sift, if called for) the dry ingredients in a bowl or a large measuring cup, and mix the milk, buttermilk, or other liquid together with the extract in a separate measuring cup. When adding the wet and dry ingredients, do so alternately, in three parts, beating after each addition. The ingredients should be blended thoroughly and the batter should be smooth, but be sure not to overbeat or the cake will lose its light texture. Remember to use a rubber spatula to scrape down the batter from the sides and the bottom of the bowl, making sure the ingredients are well blended throughout the mixing process.

When dividing the batter between the prepared pans, you can use a measuring cup if you like to ensure that you have an equal amount of batter in each pan, and your rubber spatula to spread the batter evenly.

It is best to bake cake layers in the center of the oven, placing the pans on the same rack if possible, but not touching.

ICING

Before icing, be sure that the cake layers are completely cool. Icing will not stick to a warm cake, and a warm cake becomes soggy if iced.

Be sure to brush any crumbs off the sides of the cake layers and place the layers top side up (pan side down) on a level surface. If any of the layers are uneven, you can slice off the top using a serrated knife.

The best way to frost a layer cake is by frosting between the layers first and then frosting the top and sides of the cake. If you make sure to keep plenty of icing on your spatula, the whole frosting process will go more smoothly. Keep in mind that this is one of those things that gets easier with practice.

COOKIES

Try using a small ice cream scoop (one that measures approximately 1 tablespoon in capacity) instead of a spoon for measuring your cookies. The ice cream scoop gives you even, rounded cookies that hold their shape well while baking and, obviously, makes all the cookies the same size. (Keep in mind that if you make the cookies much smaller or larger than 1 tablespoon, you must adjust the baking time accordingly.)

Second, if it's summertime and it's really hot, and your cookie dough seems too soft, put the dough in the fridge for fifteen to twenty minutes before scooping. If you bake cookies with dough that is too soft, your cookies will spread out too much during baking.

Third, for evenly browned cookies bake only one sheet of cookies at a time on the center rack of the oven.

Last, the most common problem people seem to have is that they wait too long to take the cookies out of the oven. Pay attention to the recommended baking time. The right time to take cookies out of the oven is when they look almost the way you'd like them to look but still slightly underdone. They may look a little underdone, but cookies continue to bake after they come out of the oven.

PIES

With just a little practice, a golden, flaky piecrust is not difficult to achieve. Although conventional wisdom dictates the use of chilled shortening or butter, using unchilled vegetable shortening results in a dough that is very easy to handle and produces a consistently flaky texture. Crisco butter flavor shortening gives the ideal butter flavor but, again, keeps the flakiness that people love. (By the way, using Crisco sticks makes for really easy measuring.)

Most important, if you have a pastry blender, use that instead of a food processor or standing mixer for making pies because it's so easy to overwork the dough when using these methods. Start out with the flour in a bowl, then add the shortening, cut into about half-inch pieces. Using the pastry blender, work in the shortening until the mixture resembles coarse crumbs (at this point the shortening should be pea-size). Sprinkle the *ice cold* water, by tablespoons, over the flour mixture, stirring it in gently with a fork. Be sure not to overwork the dough. Shape the dough into a ball. (If you're making a double-crust pie, divide the dough into two disks, wrap one in waxed paper, and set aside.) Place your dough on a lightly floured piece of waxed paper, flatten the dough gently with the palm of your hand, and sprinkle the top lightly with flour. Using a lightly floured rolling pin, roll out the dough from the center evenly in all directions. If the dough sticks to the rolling pin, dust it lightly with more flour. Be careful to use only as much flour as is necessary to roll out the dough, keeping in mind that adding too much flour during the rolling-out process will produce a dry, tough crust. Lay your glass pie dish facedown on top of the circle of dough, flip the pan over, gently pressing the dough into the pan, and then remove the waxed paper.

Trim the dough, leaving a half inch around the edge. If you are making a single-crust pie, tuck the overhanging pastry dough underneath itself and crimp. If you are making a double-crust pie, add the filling, mounding it in the center. Then roll out the second disk, lift the waxed paper with the dough, flip it over the filling, and remove the waxed paper. Trim the edges of the dough and pinch together the top and bottom crusts.

CHEESECAKES

The most frustrating thing about cheesecakes is the tendency for cracks to appear in the cake. The most important thing you can do to avoid these surface cracks is to not over-whip the cream cheese, because this can cause too much air to be incorporated into the batter. Be sure to set the mixer on the lowest speed and to beat the cream cheese until very smooth before adding the other ingredients. Then, when adding the other ingredients, mix only until well incorporated. Extremes in temperature can also lead to surface cracks. Avoid opening the oven door as much as possible while baking, and cool the cheesecake gradually in an oven that has been turned off.

The second most frustrating thing is not being quite sure when the cake is actually done. Even the most experienced baker still stands pondering in front of the oven, jiggling the pan, trying to make sure it's completely cooked yet still perfectly creamy. You can set the timer for an hour, but after that it's really practice and a good judgment call—there's just no fancy advice to give.

NOTE: If you would like to make individual-size cheesecakes, which were so popular at the bakery, divide the cheesecake batter into twelve 3 x 3-inch cheesecake pans with removeable bottoms, and bake for 25 to 30 minutes, or until the edges are set and the center moves only slightly.

A FEW LAST WORDS . . .

Be sure to check that your oven temperature is correct, and if you're not sure, use an oven thermometer. Many ovens are off by twenty-five degrees or more, which of course significantly alters your baking time.

Be sure that the oven is preheated to the proper temperature so that your batter is not sitting in the pan or pans at room temperature, waiting to go into the oven. Once the leavening agent is mixed into the batter it is important to get it right into the oven to start baking.

The time to arrange the oven racks to the right level for whatever you're baking is *before* you preheat the oven—not when you're ready to bake your dessert. (Too much heat escapes while you're rearranging the racks if you wait to do it then.)

If it's the first time you're attempting a recipe and you are uncertain of the baking time, test the dessert several times toward the end of the recommended time.

If you do a lot of baking (or cooking) with nuts, it's a great time saver to toast the nuts in advance so that they're ready anytime you need them for a recipe. If you have the oven on at 350 degrees for something you're making, take the opportunity to put in a pan of nuts to toast at the same time.

Always use large eggs for baking. It is important to realize that an egg is a liquid ingredient, and substituting extra-large or jumbo eggs will throw off the balance of a recipe.

Always use unsalted butter, not margarine or vegetable shortening (unless shortening is specifically called for in the recipe).

Always use pure vanilla extract, not imitation, which can taste tinny and artificial.

If you would like to make the breakfast buns, like we used to do at the bakery, use a bun pan (which has straight sides) instead of a large muffin pan. Bun pans are available in two sizes from King Arthur Flour, at www.kingarthurflour.com.

MUFFINS, BREAKFAST BUNS, AND QUICK BREADS

Corn Muffins

In pursuit of the perfect corn muffin, we think we've got the right proportion of ingredients that create a light, moist, and not-too-sweet version of this traditional breakfast favorite. Maybe that's why customers called them the best corn muffins in town!

1 ¼ cups yellow cornmeal
1 ¼ cups all-purpose flour
⅓ cup sugar
1 tablespoon baking powder
1 teaspoon salt

2 large eggs, lightly beaten
1 ½ cups milk
¾ cup (1 ½ sticks) unsalted butter,
    melted and cooled slightly

Preheat oven to 350 degrees.

Grease well 9 cups of a 12-cup muffin tin.

In a large bowl, mix together the dry ingredients, making a well in the center. Stir in the liquid ingredients until just combined, being careful not to overmix. The batter may be lumpy.

Fill the muffin cups about three-quarters full. Bake for 18–20 minutes until lightly golden or a cake tester inserted into center of muffin comes out with moist crumbs attached. Do not overbake.

MAKES 9 MUFFINS

Raspberry Cream Cheese Breakfast Buns

These buns were our most popular breakfast item at the bakery since the first day we opened our doors. The flavors of the cream cheese and the preserves work really well together.

BUN

1¾ cups all-purpose flour
1 teaspoon baking powder
½ teaspoon baking soda
¼ teaspoon salt
½ pound (one 8-ounce package)
   cream cheese, softened
½ cup (1 stick) unsalted butter,
   softened

1 cup sugar
2 large eggs, at room temperature
¼ cup milk
½ teaspoon vanilla extract

TOPPING

½ cup raspberry preserves

GARNISH

Confectioners' sugar

Preheat oven to 350 degrees.

Grease and lightly flour 9 bun pans or large muffin cups.

In a small bowl, combine the flour, baking powder, baking soda, and salt. Set aside.

In a large bowl, on the medium speed of an electric mixer, beat together the cream cheese, butter, and sugar until smooth, about 3 minutes. Add the eggs and beat well. Add the dry ingredients in two parts, alternating with the milk and vanilla. Spoon the batter into the bun pans or muffin cups, filling them about two-thirds full. Drop 3 small dollops (about a teaspoonful each) of raspberry preserves onto the top of each bun and, using the tip of a sharp knife, swirl the preserves into the batter, forming a decorative pattern. Bake for 25–30 minutes, or until a cake tester inserted in the center of the bun comes out clean.

Allow the buns to cool for about 30 minutes before sprinkling with confectioners' sugar and serving.

MAKES 9 BUNS

Banana Bread
with Coconut and Pecans

Allysa was never a big banana bread fan until the idea of adding coconut came to her one afternoon and inspired this recipe, which turned out wonderfully. It's surprisingly good with a little salted butter as well as plain.

3 cups flour
1½ teaspoons baking soda
¾ teaspoon cinnamon
¾ teaspoon salt
¾ cup canola oil
1½ cups sugar
3 large eggs, at room temperature, well beaten

1½ teaspoons vanilla extract
1½ cups mashed ripe bananas
¾ cup sour cream
1½ cups coarsely chopped toasted pecans (see Note)
¾ cup sweetened shredded coconut

NOTE: To toast the pecans, place on a baking sheet in a 350-degree oven for 15 minutes, or until lightly browned and fragrant.

Preheat oven to 350 degrees.

Grease and lightly flour a 10-inch tube pan.

In a medium-size bowl, sift together the flour, baking soda, cinnamon, and salt. Set aside.

In a large bowl, on the medium speed of an electric mixer, beat together the oil and sugar. Add the eggs and vanilla, and beat well. Add the bananas and sour cream, and mix well. Add the dry ingredients and mix until just combined. Stir in the pecans and coconut. Pour the batter into the prepared pan. Bake for 60–70 minutes, or until a cake tester inserted into the center of the bread comes out with moist crumbs attached. Let cool for at least 1 hour before removing from the pan and serving.

MAKES ONE 10-INCH CAKE

Dried Cherry Crumb Buns

Dried cherries give a new twist to the traditional breakfast crumb bun, and you don't need to worry about their being in season. At the bakery we substituted fresh apples for the cherries at times, and even chocolate chips for a slightly sweeter version.

BUNS
2 cups all-purpose flour
1 tablespoon baking powder
¼ teaspoon salt
⅛ teaspoon cinnamon
½ cup (1 stick) butter, softened
1 cup sugar
2 large eggs, at room temperature

1 teaspoon vanilla extract
1 cup buttermilk
1½ cups dried cherries

TOPPING
2¼ cups all-purpose flour
1½ cups unpacked light brown sugar
1 cup (2 sticks) unsalted butter,
    softened and cut into small pieces

Preheat oven to 325 degrees.

Grease and flour 16 large muffin cups.

To make the buns: In a medium-size bowl, sift together the flour, the baking powder, the salt, and the cinnamon. Set aside.

In a large bowl, on the low speed of an electric mixer, cream the butter and the sugar until fluffy, about 3 minutes. Add the eggs one at a time, beating well after each addition. Beat in the vanilla. Add the dry ingredients alternately with the buttermilk, in three parts, beating well after each addition. Stir the dried cherries into the batter. Spoon the batter into the muffin cups.

To prepare the topping: In a medium-size bowl, mix the flour and the brown sugar. Using a pastry blender, cut in the butter until the mixture resembles coarse crumbs.

Sprinkle topping over buns, being sure to keep crumbs within muffin cups; otherwise they are difficult to remove.

Bake for 20–25 minutes until lightly golden or until a cake tester inserted into center of bun comes out clean.

MAKES 16 BUNS

Oatmeal Muffins

Here's an old-fashioned breakfast treat. The kids will never know they're eating their oatmeal!

2 cups rolled oats (not quick-cooking oats)
1 ½ cups milk
1 ½ cups all-purpose flour
1 tablespoon baking powder
½ teaspoon salt

¼ teaspoon cinnamon
2 large eggs, lightly beaten
½ cup firmly packed light brown sugar
½ cup (1 stick) unsalted butter, melted and cooled slightly
1 teaspoon vanilla extract

Preheat oven to 400 degrees.

Grease well a 12-cup muffin tin.

In a medium-size bowl, mix the oats and the milk and set aside for 10 minutes.

Meanwhile, in a large bowl, mix together the dry ingredients, making a well in the center. Stir in the liquid ingredients and the oatmeal mixture until just combined, being careful not to overmix. Batter may be lumpy.

Fill the muffin cups about three-quarters full. Bake for 16–18 minutes until lightly golden or a cake taster inserted into center of muffin comes out with moist crumbs attached. Do not overbake.

MAKES 12 MUFFINS

Sour Cream Breakfast Buns

The comforting smell of brown sugar and cinnamon made these buns a customer favorite. When our busy morning patrons grabbed one on the go, we liked to think they'd have a peaceful moment in their hectic day as they enjoyed it.

BUN
3 cups all-purpose flour
1½ teaspoons baking powder
1½ teaspoons baking soda
¾ cup (1½ sticks) unsalted butter,
    softened
1½ cups sugar
3 large eggs, at room temperature

1½ teaspoons vanilla extract
1½ cups sour cream

TOPPING
1⅓ cups firmly packed light brown
    sugar
2 cups coarsely chopped pecans
2 teaspoons cinnamon

Preheat oven to 350 degrees.

Grease 18 large muffin cups.

To make the buns: In a medium-size bowl, sift together the flour, the baking powder, and the baking soda. Set aside.

In a large bowl, on the low speed of an electric mixer, cream the butter with the sugar until fluffy, about 3 minutes. Add the eggs one at a time, beating well after each addition. Beat in the vanilla. Add the dry ingredients and mix until just combined. Mix in the sour cream. Spoon the batter into the muffin cups.

To make the topping: In a small bowl, mix the brown sugar, the pecans, and the cinnamon. Sprinkle the topping evenly (and generously) over the buns.

Bake for 20–25 minutes or until a cake tester inserted into center of bun comes out clean.

MAKES 18 BUNS

Poppy Seed Bread

Here's a great morning quick bread that can be enjoyed any time of day. We chose to make this in a tube pan so you'll be sure to have extra on hand.

2 ½ cups all-purpose flour
1 ½ teaspoons baking powder
¼ teaspoon salt
1 ¼ cups vegetable oil
1 ¼ cups sugar

3 large eggs, at room temperature
1 cup evaporated milk
⅓ cup milk
1 tablespoon vanilla extract
¼ cup poppy seeds

Preheat oven to 375 degrees.

Grease and flour a 10-inch tube pan.

In a large bowl, sift together the flour, the baking powder, and the salt. Set aside.

In a large bowl, mix the oil and the sugar. Add the eggs one at a time, beating after each addition. Add the evaporated milk, the milk, and the vanilla. Add the dry ingredients and mix well. Stir in the poppy seeds.

Pour the batter into the prepared tube pan. Bake for 45 minutes or until a cake tester inserted into center of bread comes out with moist crumbs attached. Let cool for 20 minutes before serving.

MAKES 1 BREAD

Pear Streusel Breakfast Buns

A really nice, not-too-sweet breakfast treat. You can substitute apples for the pears if you like.

STREUSEL TOPPING
1 cup firmly packed light brown sugar
1 ½ teaspoons cinnamon
4 tablespoons (½ stick) unsalted butter, softened and cut into small pieces
1 ½ cups chopped walnuts

BUNS
1 ½ cups all-purpose flour
¼ teaspoon baking soda
¼ teaspoon salt
¾ cup (1 ½ sticks) unsalted butter, softened
1 cup sugar
3 eggs, at room temperature
6 tablespoons milk
1 teaspoon vanilla extract
1 ½ cups coarsely chopped peeled pears

Preheat oven to 350 degrees.

Grease and lightly flour 12 bun pans or large muffin cups.

To make the topping: In a medium-size bowl, combine the brown sugar and cinnamon. Using a pastry blender, cut in the butter until the mixture resembles coarse crumbs. Add the walnuts, and using your hands, toss until the ingredients are well combined. Set aside.

To make the buns: In a small bowl, combine the flour, baking soda, and salt. Set aside.

In a large bowl, on the medium speed of an electric mixer, cream the butter until smooth. Add the sugar gradually and beat until fluffy, about 3 minutes. Add the eggs, one at a time, beating well after each addition.

Add the dry ingredients in two parts, alternating with the milk and vanilla, beating until well incorporated. Stir in pears. Spoon the batter into the bun pans or muffin cups. Sprinkle the topping over the buns, being sure to keep the crumbs within the muffin cups (otherwise the buns are difficult to remove from the pan).

Bake for 20–25 minutes, or until a cake tester inserted in the center of the bun comes out clean.

MAKES 12 BUNS

Blueberry Muffins

Nothing makes a cheerful morning like the smell of fresh muffins baking in the kitchen. These muffins originally called for whole milk, but substituting buttermilk really adds a special tangy moistness. Our friend Johnny Parker would have never thought about getting on a plane to go away on business without at least half a dozen of these in his carry-on!

3 cups all-purpose flour
¾ cup plus 1 tablespoon
    (for sprinkling) sugar
1½ tablespoons baking powder
¾ teaspoon salt
2 large eggs, lightly beaten

1½ cups buttermilk
6 tablespoons (¾ stick) unsalted
    butter, melted and cooled slightly
1½ teaspoons vanilla extract
1½ cups blueberries, lightly coated
    with flour

Preheat oven to 350 degrees.

Grease well a 12-cup muffin tin.

In a large bowl, mix together the dry ingredients, making a well in the center. Stir in the liquid ingredients until just combined, being careful not to overmix. Batter may be lumpy. Gently fold the blueberries into the batter.

Fill the muffin cups about three-quarters full. Lightly sprinkle with the reserved tablespoon of sugar. Bake for 20–22 minutes until lightly golden or a cake taster inserted into center of muffin comes out with moist crumbs attached. Do not overbake.

MAKES 12 MUFFINS

Cranberry Orange Bread

Jennifer and good friend Peggy Williams used to bake this every year at Thanksgiving to bring to their family dinners. People always asked us for the recipe, and we've decided to share it with you.

2 cups all-purpose flour
1 cup plus 1 tablespoon
    (for sprinkling) sugar
1 ½ teaspoons baking powder
½ teaspoon baking soda
1 teaspoon salt

¾ cup plus 2 tablespoons orange juice
1 large egg, at room temperature
1 tablespoon grated orange zest
2 tablespoons unsalted butter, melted
1 cup whole cranberries, coarsely
    chopped

Preheat oven to 350 degrees.

Grease and flour a 9 x 5 x 3-inch loaf pan.

In a medium-size bowl, combine the flour, the sugar, the baking powder, the baking soda, and the salt. Set aside.

In a large bowl, mix the orange juice, the egg, the zest, and the butter. Add the dry ingredients and mix well. Add the cranberries and combine.

Pour the batter into prepared pan. Sprinkle the top with the reserved tablespoon of sugar. Add a few cranberries on top for decoration if desired. Bake for about 1 hour or until a cake tester inserted into center of loaf comes out clean. Let cool for 20 minutes before serving.

VARIATION: Add ½ cup poppy seeds instead of cranberries for a delicious orange-poppy bread.

MAKES 1 LOAF

Cream Cheese Crumb Buns

This recipe was inspired, believe it or not, by the Freihofer-brand crumb cheese coffee cake. A number of years back, some of the staff were at Allysa's house (when she first moved and didn't yet have a kitchen), and we were eating the Freihofer cake (right out of the box, of course) and said, "This is really good. We could make this at the bakery." So Allysa came up with this recipe.

CREAM CHEESE FILLING
½ pound (one 8-ounce package)
    cream cheese, softened
3 tablespoons unsalted butter,
    softened
2 tablespoons sugar
1 large egg yolk, at room temperature
½ teaspoon vanilla extract

CRUMB TOPPING
1½ cups all-purpose flour
1 cup firmly packed light brown sugar
2 teaspoons baking powder
½ cup (1 stick) unsalted butter,
    softened and cut into small pieces

BUNS
1½ cups all-purpose flour
1 teaspoon baking powder
¼ teaspoon salt
½ cup solid vegetable shortening
½ cup sugar
2 large eggs, at room temperature
½ cup milk

Preheat oven to 350 degrees.

Grease and lightly flour 16 bun pans or large muffin cups.

To make the filling: In a medium-size bowl, beat the cream cheese and butter until smooth and creamy. Add the sugar, egg yolk, and vanilla, and beat well. Set aside.

To make the topping: In a large bowl, mix together the flour, sugar, and baking powder. Using a pastry blender, cut in the butter until the mixture resembles coarse crumbs. Set aside.

To make the buns: In a small bowl, combine the flour, baking powder, and salt. Set aside.

In a large bowl, on the medium speed of an electric mixer, beat together the shortening and sugar until smooth. Add the eggs, one at a time, beating well after each addi-

(continued)

tion. Add the dry ingredients, in two parts, alternating with the milk and beating until well incorporated. Spoon the batter into the bun pans or muffin cups. Bake for 10 minutes.

Remove from the oven, and working quickly but carefully, place a tablespoon of the cream cheese filling in the center of each bun and press it down gently with the back of the spoon. Sprinkle the crumb topping over the cream cheese, covering the entire top of the bun and being sure to keep the crumbs within the muffin cups (otherwise the buns are difficult to remove from the pan). Return to the oven and bake for an additional 13 minutes. (Do not use a cake tester to check for doneness—it will only come out with cream cheese filling attached!)

Allow to cool for 30 minutes before serving. These are best when eaten warm with the filling still a little gooey.

MAKES 16 BUNS

Chocolate Chip Peanut Banana Loaf

It's the peanuts that add a bit of crunch and texture to this breakfast and teatime favorite. A healthy treat that's not overly sweet—enjoy!

⅓ cup (5⅓ tablespoons) unsalted butter, softened
½ cup sugar
2 large eggs, at room temperature
1½ cups mashed ripe bananas

⅓ cup milk
2 cups sifted self-rising flour
½ cup finely chopped, unsalted peanuts
¾ cup chocolate chips

Preheat oven to 350 degrees.

Grease and flour a 9 x 5 x 3 inch loaf pan.

In a large bowl, on the low speed of an electric mixer, cream the butter and the sugar until fluffy, about 2–3 minutes. Add the eggs one at a time. Add the mashed bananas and the milk. Mix in the sifted flour until well combined. Stir in the peanuts and the chocolate chips. Pour the batter into prepared pan and bake for 45–55 minutes or until a cake tester inserted into center of loaf comes out clean.

Let cool for 20 minutes before serving.

MAKES 1 LOAF

Apple Pecan Quick Bread

Here's a terrific quick bread for any time of day. If there's any left over, this bread is great when lightly toasted and spread with some cream cheese. For an added tart flavor, substitute cranberries for half the apples.

1¾ cups all-purpose flour
¾ cup sugar
1 tablespoon baking powder
½ teaspoon salt
⅔ cup orange juice
⅓ cup (5⅓ tablespoons) unsalted
    butter, melted and cooled slightly

2 large eggs, lightly beaten
1½ cups coarsely chopped Golden
    Delicious apples
½ cup coarsely chopped
    pecans

Preheat oven to 350 degrees.

Grease a 9 x 5 x 3-inch loaf pan.

In a large bowl, sift together the flour, the sugar, the baking powder, and the salt, making a well in the center. Set aside. Stir in the liquid ingredients until just combined, being careful not to overmix. Gently stir in the apples and the pecans. Pour the batter into prepared pan and bake for 50–60 minutes or until a cake tester inserted into center of loaf comes out with moist crumbs attached. Do not overbake.

MAKES 1 LOAF

Glazed Breakfast Buns

This delicate bun topped with a streusel glaze will definitely start your day off right.

BUNS
3 cups all-purpose flour
½ teaspoon baking soda
½ teaspoon salt
1 ½ cups (3 sticks) unsalted butter, softened
2 ¼ cups sugar
6 large eggs, at room temperature
¾ cup milk
2 teaspoons vanilla extract

GLAZE
1 ½ cups confectioners' sugar
3 tablespoons water

GARNISH
1 ½ cups coarsely chopped pecans or walnuts (or nut of your choice)

Preheat oven to 350 degrees.

Grease and flour 18 large muffin cups.

To make the buns: In a medium-size bowl, combine the flour, the baking soda, and the salt. Set aside.

In a large bowl, on the low speed of an electric mixer, cream the butter with the sugar until fluffy, about 3 minutes. Add the eggs one at a time, beating well after each addition. Add the dry ingredients alternating with the milk and the vanilla, in three parts, beating until well incorporated. Spoon the batter into the muffin cups. Bake for 25–28 minutes or until a cake tester inserted into center of bun comes out clean. Remove from oven and allow buns to cool for about 30 minutes.

To make the glaze: In a small bowl, stir together the sugar and the water until smooth. Drizzle the glaze over the buns and sprinkle generously with chopped nuts.

MAKES 18 BUNS

Zucchini Walnut Bread

This is a recipe that Allysa has been making since she was a teenager, and she's tweaked it here and there over the years. If you have a vegetable garden and can pick your own fresh squash, it makes all the difference.

1 cup all-purpose flour
1 teaspoon baking soda
½ teaspoon baking powder
½ teaspoon salt
½ teaspoon cinnamon
½ cup vegetable oil (preferably canola)

¾ cup sugar
2 large eggs, at room temperature
½ teaspoon vanilla extract
1 cup shredded zucchini
  (including skin)
¾ cup chopped walnuts

Preheat oven to 350 degrees.

Grease and flour a 9 x 5 x 3-inch loaf pan.

In a small bowl, combine the flour, baking soda, baking powder, salt, and cinnamon. Set aside.

In a large bowl, on the medium speed of an electric mixer, beat together the oil, sugar, eggs, and vanilla until light and thick, about 3 minutes. Stir in the zucchini.

Add the dry ingredients and mix until just combined. Stir in the walnuts.

Pour the batter into the prepared pan. Place on a baking sheet and bake for 50–60 minutes, or until a cake tester inserted in the center of the loaf comes out with moist crumbs attached. Let cool for at least 1 hour before serving.

MAKES 1 LOAF

COFFEE CAKES
AND
BUNDT CAKES

Blueberry Coffee Cake with Vanilla Glaze

This light and moist coffee cake is simple to prepare and makes a good addition to breakfast or brunch.

Cake

2 cups all-purpose flour
2 teaspoons baking powder
1 teaspoon salt
⅔ cup vegetable oil (preferably canola)
1 cup sugar
2 large eggs, at room temperature
1 cup milk

1 teaspoon vanilla extract
½ cups fresh blueberries, lightly coated with flour

Vanilla Glaze

1 ¼ cups confectioners' sugar, sifted
¼ cup heavy cream
½ teaspoon vanilla extract

Preheat oven to 325 degrees.

Grease and lightly flour a 10-inch tube pan.

In a small bowl, sift together the flour, baking powder, and salt. Set aside.

In a large bowl, on the medium speed of an electric mixer, beat together the oil, sugar, and eggs until light and thick, about 3 minutes. Add the dry ingredients in three parts, alternating with the milk and vanilla, beating after each addition until smooth. Fold in the blueberries. Pour the batter into the prepared pan and bake for 60–70 minutes, or until a cake tester inserted in the center of the cake comes out clean. Let the cake cool in the pan for 1 hour. Remove from the pan and cool completely on a wire rack.

To make the vanilla glaze: In the top of a double boiler, over barely simmering water, combine the sugar, cream, and vanilla. Stir until the ingredients are well blended, about 2 minutes. Pour into a glass measuring cup and cover until ready to use. When the cake is completely cool, drizzle the glaze decoratively over the cake. Allow the glaze to set for 1 hour before slicing and serving the cake.

MAKES ONE 10-INCH CAKE

Lemon Vanilla Bundt Cake

Jennifer's mom, Susanne, developed this pound cake recipe about twenty-five years ago. It's a surefire hit every time it's served, and there's never an Appel get-together without it. The secret to the tender crumb is the club soda. Kudos to Mom!

1 ½ cups (3 sticks) unsalted butter,
    softened
3 cups sugar
5 large eggs, at room temperature

3 cups all-purpose flour
¾ cup club soda (not seltzer)
2 tablespoons vanilla extract
1 ½ tablespoons grated lemon zest

Preheat oven to 350 degrees.

Grease and lightly flour a 10-inch Bundt pan.

In a large bowl, on the medium speed of an electric mixer, cream the butter and the sugar until fluffy, about 3 minutes. Add the eggs one at a time, mixing well after each addition. Add the flour in thirds, alternating with the club soda, beating after each addition until smooth. Add the vanilla and the lemon zest and mix well. Pour the batter into prepared pan and bake 70–80 minutes until golden brown or a cake tester inserted into center of cake comes out clean. Let cake cool in pan for 20 minutes. Remove from pan and cool completely on wire rack.

VARIATION: For an equally delicious cake, try this as a marble cake. Pour ⅔ of the batter into prepared pan, then pour ⅓ cup unsweetened cocoa powder on top. Gently press the powder down into the batter with a large spoon. Pour in the remaining batter. Baking time should remain the same.

MAKES ONE 10-INCH CAKE

Pear Pecan Cake

This recipe was handed down to our friend Debra Davis from her Texan grand-mother, Winifred Crawford. The cake can also be made with sweet or tart apples and with or without the glaze. You won't be disappointed with any variation.

Cake
3 cups all-purpose flour
2 cups sugar
½ teaspoon baking soda
½ teaspoon salt
1 cup plus 2 tablespoons vegetable oil
3 large eggs, at room temperature

1 teaspoon vanilla extract
2 Bosc pears, cut into 1-inch pieces
   (about 2 cups)
1 cup coarsely chopped pecans

Glaze
1½ cups confectioners' sugar
3 tablespoons water

Preheat oven to 350 degrees.

Lightly grease a 10-inch tube pan.

To make the cake: In a large bowl, sift together the flour, the sugar, the baking soda, and the salt, making a well in the center. Stir in the oil, the eggs, and the vanilla. Stir in the pears and the pecans. Spoon the batter into prepared pan. Bake for 60–70 minutes or until a cake tester inserted into center of cake comes out clean. Let cake cool in pan for 20 minutes. Remove from pan and cool completely on wire rack.

To make the glaze: In a small bowl, stir together the sugar and the water until smooth. Drizzle decoratively over cooled cake. Garnish with pecans if desired.

MAKES ONE 10-INCH CAKE

Chocolate Amaretto Bundt Cake

After tasting a delicious cake at another bakery, Jennifer was so impressed that she developed this recipe from scratch to try to match their confection. We think you'll love this unbelievably moist and chocolaty cake.

2 cups all-purpose flour
1 teaspoon baking soda
1 cup (2 sticks) unsalted butter, softened
1 cup sugar
1 cup firmly packed light brown sugar
4 large eggs, at room temperature

6 ounces semisweet chocolate, melted (see Note)
1 cup milk
3 teaspoons almond extract
1 teaspoon vanilla extract
4 tablespoons amaretto-flavored liqueur

NOTE: To melt chocolate, place in a double boiler over simmering water on low heat for approximately 5–10 minutes. Stir occasionally until completely smooth and no pieces of chocolate remain. Remove from heat and let cool for 5–10 minutes.

Preheat oven to 350 degrees.

Grease and lightly flour a 10-inch Bundt pan.

In a medium-size bowl, sift together the flour and the baking soda. Set aside.

In a large bowl, on the medium speed of an electric mixer, cream the butter and the sugars until fluffy, about 3 minutes. Add the eggs one at a time, mixing well after each addition. Add the chocolate, mixing until well incorporated. Add the dry ingredients in thirds, alternating with the milk and the extracts, beating after each addition until smooth. Add the liqueur and mix well. Pour the batter into prepared pan and bake 45–50 minutes or until a cake tester inserted into center of cake comes out clean. Let cake cool in pan for 20 minutes. Remove from pan and cool completely on wire rack.

MAKES ONE 10-INCH CAKE

Apple Cake with Cinnamon Sugar Topping

Allysa loves to get up really early when she has guests visiting for the weekend and make this coffee cake. Using canned sliced apples makes it extremely easy to prepare, and it's out of the oven before everyone else wakes up for breakfast.

2 cups all-purpose flour
2 teaspoons baking powder
1 teaspoon salt
⅔ cup vegetable oil (preferably canola)
1 cup sugar
2 large eggs, at room temperature

1 cup milk
1 teaspoon vanilla extract
One 20-ounce can sliced apples, drained and patted dry
½ cup sugar mixed with 1 teaspoon cinnamon

Preheat oven to 325 degrees.

Grease and lightly flour a 10-inch tube pan.

In a small bowl, sift together the flour, baking powder, and salt. Set aside.

In a large bowl, on the medium speed of an electric mixer, beat together the oil, sugar, and eggs until light and thick, about 3 minutes. Add the dry ingredients in three parts, alternating with the milk and vanilla, beating after each addition until smooth. In a separate small bowl, toss the apples with half of the cinnamon-sugar mixture, then stir half of the apples into the batter. Pour the batter into the prepared pan. Drop the remaining apples on top of the batter and sprinkle with the remaining cinnamon sugar. Bake for 60–70 minutes, or until a cake tester inserted in the center of the cake comes out clean. Let the cake cool in the pan for 1 hour, then remove from the pan and cool completely on a wire rack.

MAKES ONE 10-INCH CAKE

Poppy Seed Coffee Cake

Despite the belief of many New Yorkers, poppy seeds aren't found just on bagels. Try this yummy and unique version of an old standby the next time the folks pop in for coffee and cake. As a variation, try using prune or apricot filling in place of the poppy filling.

COFFEE CAKE
1 ½ cups all-purpose flour
1 teaspoon baking powder
¼ teaspoon salt
2 eggs, separated, at room
    temperature (see Note)
½ cup solid vegetable shortening
½ cup sugar

½ cup milk
1 twelve-ounce can poppy filling

TOPPING
6 tablespoons all-purpose flour
¼ cup brown sugar
½ teaspoon baking powder
2 tablespoons unsalted butter,
    softened

NOTE: It is best to separate the eggs when cold and then allow them to come to room temperature before proceeding with the recipe.

Preheat oven to 350 degrees.

Line an 8 x 8 x 2-inch square baking pan with waxed paper.

To prepare the coffee cake: In a medium-size bowl, sift together the flour, the baking powder, and the salt. Set aside.

In a small bowl, lightly beat the egg yolks, about 1 minute.

In a large bowl, on the low speed of an electric mixer, cream the shortening and the sugar until fluffy, about 2–3 minutes. Add the egg yolks. Add the dry ingredients in two parts, alternating with the milk. In a separate bowl, on the high speed of an electric mixer, beat the egg whites until stiff peaks form. Gently fold the egg whites into the batter. Batter will be thick and doughlike.

Meanwhile, prepare the topping: In a small bowl, mix together the flour, the brown sugar, and the baking powder. Using a pastry blender, cut in the butter until the mixture resembles coarse crumbs.

Pour the batter into prepared pan. Make indentations with the back of a spoon and press teaspoonfuls of the poppy filling into each indentation. Sprinkle the topping over cake. Bake 40–45 minutes or until a cake tester comes out with moist crumbs attached. Do not overbake.

Allow to cool for 20 minutes before cutting and serving.

MAKES 1 CAKE

Chocolate Sour Cream Cake with Chocolate Chips

This simple but chocolaty cake has a nice sour-cream tang to it. It's the kind of cake that sits on the kitchen table to be shared with visiting neighbors over a cup of coffee.

3 cups plus 2 tablespoons all-purpose flour
1 ½ teaspoons baking soda
¼ teaspoon salt
3 ounces unsweetened chocolate, coarsely chopped
1 tablespoon instant espresso
1 ½ cups boiling water

¾ cup (1 ½ sticks) unsalted butter, softened
2 ⅔ cups firmly packed light brown sugar
2 large eggs, at room temperature
1 ½ teaspoons vanilla extract
¾ cup sour cream
⅔ cup miniature chocolate chips

Preheat oven to 325 degrees.

Grease and lightly flour a 10-inch tube pan.

In a large bowl, sift together the flour, the baking soda, and the salt. Set aside.

Place the chocolate and the espresso in a medium-size bowl. Add the boiling water and stir until chocolate is melted. Set aside to cool for 5 or 10 minutes.

Meanwhile, in a large bowl, on the low speed of an electric mixer, cream the butter with the sugar until fluffy, about 3 minutes. Add the eggs one at a time, beating well after each addition. Add the vanilla. Gradually add the dry ingredients, beating only until smooth. Add the sour cream. Add the chocolate mixture in three parts, beating after each addition. Stir in the chocolate chips. Pour the batter into prepared pan and bake for 70–80 minutes or until a cake tester inserted into center of cake comes out clean.

Let cake cool in pan for 20 minutes. Remove from pan and cool completely on wire rack.

MAKES ONE 10-INCH CAKE

Brown Sugar Pecan Cake

Allysa loves cake that is not too sweet or too fancy and can be eaten at the kitchen table in the afternoon with tea or coffee. This can also be served with whipped cream if you like.

2 cups cake flour (not self-rising)

2 teaspoons baking powder

½ teaspoon salt

¾ cup (1 ½ sticks) unsalted butter, softened

1 ½ cups firmly packed light brown sugar

2 large eggs, at room temperature

1 cup milk

1 teaspoon vanilla extract

1 ½ cups chopped toasted pecans (see Note)

NOTE: To toast the pecans, place on a baking sheet in a 350-degree oven for 15 minutes, or until lightly browned and fragrant.

Preheat oven to 325 degrees.

Grease and lightly flour a 10-inch tube pan.

In a small bowl, sift together the flour, baking powder, and salt. Set aside.

In a large bowl, on the medium speed of an electric mixer, cream the butter until smooth. Add the sugar gradually and beat until fluffy, about 3 minutes. Add the eggs, one at a time, beating well after each addition. Add the dry ingredients in three parts, alternating with the milk and vanilla, beating after each addition until smooth. Stir in 1¼ cups (reserving ¼ cup) of the pecans. Pour the batter into the prepared pan and sprinkle the remaining ¼ cup of pecans over the top.

Bake for 60–70 minutes, or until a cake tester inserted in the center of the cake comes out clean. Let the cake cool in the pan for 1 hour. Remove from the pan and cool completely on a wire rack.

MAKES ONE 10-INCH CAKE

Dump Cake

Upon hearing that we were collecting recipes for our first cookbook, customer Steven Kaplan, who is from the South, told us of a wonderful dessert his mom always made, called "dump cake." "It's the easiest thing in the world," says Kaplan, "because you just dump in all the ingredients, and out comes this terrific cake!" He sure was right!

1 twenty-one-ounce can cherry pie
    filling
1 sixteen-ounce can crushed
    pineapple, with juice
½ box white cake mix (just the plain
    mix, nothing added)

½ cup coarsely chopped pecans
½ cup (1 stick) unsalted butter,
    cut into thin slices

Preheat oven to 325 degrees.

Pour the cherry pie filling into a 13 x 9-inch glass baking dish and smooth evenly over the bottom of dish with a rubber spatula. Pour canned pineapple over the pie filling. Sprinkle the white cake mix completely over the pineapple. Place pecans evenly over cake mix. Top with slices of butter. Bake about 45 minutes or until cake appears golden brown and bubbly. Serve warm right from the dish with a dollop of whipped cream.

MAKES 1 CAKE

COOKIES

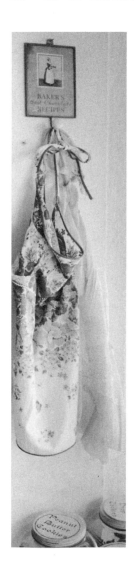

Chocolate Chip Cookies

Allysa and childhood friend Beatrice spent many hours of fun in the kitchen and came up with this tasty recipe of their own in sixth grade. It sure beats doing homework! At the bakery we sometimes add 1 cup of chopped walnuts or pecans, or substitute vanilla chips or chopped Heath Bars for the chocolate chips.

1 ½ cups all-purpose flour
1 teaspoon baking soda
½ teaspoon salt
⅔ cup (1 ⅓ sticks) unsalted butter, softened
½ cup sugar

½ cup firmly packed light brown sugar
1 large egg, at room temperature
1 teaspoon vanilla extract
½ cup miniature semisweet chocolate chips

Preheat oven to 350 degrees.

In a large bowl, combine the flour, the baking soda, and the salt. Set aside.

In a large bowl, cream the butter with the sugars until smooth, about 3 minutes. Add the egg and the vanilla and mix well. Add the flour mixture and beat thoroughly. Stir in the chocolate chips. Drop by rounded teaspoonfuls onto ungreased cookie sheets, leaving several inches between for expansion. Bake for 10–12 minutes or until lightly golden brown.

Cool the cookies on the sheets for 1 minute, then remove to a rack to cool completely.

MAKES 2–3 DOZEN COOKIES

Oatmeal Raisin Almond Cookies

Here's another old-fashioned favorite with a nutty almond crunch. They're crunch-a-licious!

2¼ cups all-purpose flour
¾ teaspoon baking soda
½ teaspoon salt
1 cup (2 sticks) unsalted butter, softened
1½ cups firmly packed light brown sugar

2 large eggs, at room temperature
1 tablespoon vanilla extract
½ teaspoon almond extract
1¼ cups rolled oats
1½ cups raisins
½ cup finely chopped toasted almonds (see Note)

NOTE: To toast almonds, place on a baking sheet in a 325-degree oven for approximately 10–15 minutes or until lightly browned and fragrant.

Preheat oven to 350 degrees.

In a large bowl, sift together the flour, the baking soda, and the salt. Set aside.

In a large bowl, cream the butter and the sugar until smooth, about 3 minutes. Add the eggs one at a time, the vanilla extract, and the almond extract and mix well. Add the oats and the flour mixture and beat thoroughly. Mix in the raisins and almonds. Chill the mixture for 30 minutes in the refrigerator before proceeding. Drop by rounded teaspoonfuls onto ungreased cookie sheets, leaving several inches between for expansion. Bake for 15–18 minutes or until lightly golden brown.

Cool the cookies on the sheets for 1 minute, then remove to a rack to cool completely.

MAKES ABOUT 3 DOZEN COOKIES

Pumpkin Walnut Cookies with Brown Butter Frosting

This spicy, cakelike cookie comes from Nancy Sinko, the mother of Barbara and Shelly, who worked at the bakery for years. Nancy frosted these cookies with a cream-cheese icing—either way, they're really good.

COOKIE
2½ cups all-purpose flour
1 tablespoon baking powder
1 teaspoon salt
1 teaspoon allspice
½ teaspoon cinnamon
¼ teaspoon ginger
4 tablespoons (½ stick) unsalted
    butter, softened
1½ cups firmly packed light brown
    sugar
2 large eggs, at room temperature

1 cup canned pumpkin puree
2 teaspoons vanilla extract
1 cup chopped walnuts

FROSTING
2 cups confectioners' sugar
3 tablespoons milk
1 teaspoon vanilla extract
3 tablespoons unsalted butter

GARNISH
Walnut halves

Preheat oven to 375 degrees.

To make the cookies: In a small bowl, combine the flour, baking powder, salt, allspice, cinnamon, and ginger. Set aside.

In a large bowl, cream the butter and sugar until evenly combined. Add the eggs, pumpkin, and vanilla, and beat well. Add the dry ingredients and mix thoroughly. Stir in the walnuts. Drop by rounded teaspoonfuls onto ungreased cookie sheets, leaving several inches between for expansion. The batter will seem extremely soft compared with most cookie doughs, but it will firm up during baking. Bake for 12 minutes. Cool the cookies on the sheets for 10–12 minutes, and then remove to a wire rack to cool completely.

To make the frosting: Place the sugar, milk, and vanilla in a small bowl. Set aside. In a small saucepan over medium-high heat, cook the butter until lightly browned,

(continued)

about 3–5 minutes. Remove from the heat, add to the other ingredients, and beat until smooth and creamy. Cover until ready to use.

When the cookies are completely cool, spread a generous amount of frosting on each cookie, and top with a walnut half. Let the icing set before stacking the cookies or they will stick together.

MAKES 4 DOZEN COOKIES

Chocolate Drop Cookies with Heath Bars, Vanilla Chips, and Pecans

Who says all chocolate chip cookies are created equal? These cookies have white chips in a deep chocolaty cookie, with toffee and pecans added to make them extra rich. Grab a glass of milk and enjoy!

2 ¼ cups all-purpose flour

⅔ cup unsweetened cocoa powder

1 teaspoon baking soda

1 teaspoon salt

1 ⅓ cups (2 ⅔ sticks) unsalted butter, softened

1 cup sugar

⅔ cup firmly packed light brown sugar

2 large eggs, at room temperature

3 tablespoons milk

1 tablespoon vanilla extract

1 ½ cups coarsely chopped pecans

4 coarsely chopped Heath Bars or chocolate-covered toffee bars (about 1 cup)

½ cup vanilla chips

Preheat oven to 350 degrees.

In a large bowl, combine the flour, the cocoa powder, the baking soda, and the salt. Set aside.

In a large bowl, cream the butter and the sugars until smooth, about 3 minutes. Add the eggs and mix well. Add the milk and the vanilla. Add the flour mixture and beat thoroughly. Stir in the pecans, the Heath Bars, and the vanilla chips. Drop by rounded teaspoonfuls onto ungreased cookie sheets, leaving several inches between for expansion. Bake for 10–12 minutes.

Cool the cookies on the sheets for 1 minute, then remove to a rack to cool completely.

MAKES ABOUT 3 DOZEN COOKIES

Oatmeal Peanut Butter Chip Cookies

After countless evenings Allysa spent standing in front of the open refrigerator, dipping freshly baked oatmeal cookies into the jar of Skippy . . .

1 cup all-purpose flour
½ teaspoon baking soda
½ teaspoon salt
¼ teaspoon cinnamon
¾ cup (1½ sticks) unsalted butter, softened
¾ cup firmly packed light brown sugar

½ cup sugar
1 large egg, at room temperature
1½ teaspoons vanilla extract
2½ cups quick-cooking oats (not regular, old-fashioned rolled oats)
1 cup peanut butter chips

Preheat oven to 350 degrees.

In a small bowl, combine the flour, baking soda, salt, and cinnamon. Set aside.

In a large bowl, cream the butter with the sugars until smooth, about 2 minutes. Add the egg and vanilla, and beat well. Add the dry ingredients and mix thoroughly. Stir in the oats and peanut butter chips. Drop by rounded teaspoonfuls onto ungreased cookie sheets, leaving several inches between for expansion. Bake for 11–13 minutes.

Cool the cookies on the sheets for 5 minutes, and then remove to a wire rack to cool completely.

MAKES 3 DOZEN COOKIES

Chocolate Covered Log Cookies

There's something so pretty and festive about these orange-scented chocolaty cookies. Roll them in a friend's favorite chopped nut for a tasty holiday gift.

1 cup (2 sticks) unsalted butter, softened
1 cup sugar
2 large eggs, at room temperature
1½ teaspoons grated orange zest
1 teaspoon vanilla extract

3¼ cups all-purpose flour
12 ounces semisweet chocolate, melted (see Note)
1 cup finely chopped nuts (such as pecans, walnuts, or nut of your choice)

NOTE: To melt chocolate, place in a double boiler over simmering water on low heat for approximately 5–10 minutes. Stir occasionally until completely smooth and no pieces of chocolate remain. Remove from heat and let cool for 5–10 minutes.

Preheat oven to 350 degrees.

In a large bowl, cream the butter until smooth, about 3 minutes. Gradually beat in the sugar and cream until fluffy. Beat in the eggs one at a time. Stir in the orange zest and the vanilla until well combined. Gradually add the flour until blended (dough will be crumbly).

Make a ball with the dough, flatten it, and then wrap in plastic and place in refrigerator for at least 1 hour (can be refrigerated overnight).

Remove the dough from refrigerator and let soften for 5–10 minutes. Taking small pieces of dough, roll them into balls and then 3-inch logs. Place logs onto ungreased cookie sheets, leaving several inches between for expansion. Bake for 10–12 minutes or until lightly golden. Cool the cookies on the sheets for 1 minute, then remove to a rack to cool completely. Meanwhile, melt the chocolate. When cookies have cooled for about 15 minutes, dip them halfway in the chocolate, then roll in the chopped nuts. Allow them to set for 15 minutes before serving.

MAKES 2½–3 DOZEN COOKIES

Toffee Pecan Drop Cookies

If you can't find the toffee pieces in your supermarket's baking section, you can substitute chopped Heath bar candy—but Allysa loves these cookies without any chocolate in them.

2 cups all-purpose flour
1 teaspoon baking soda
½ teaspoon salt
1 cup (2 sticks) unsalted butter
¾ cup firmly packed light brown sugar
¼ cup sugar

1 large egg, at room temperature
1½ teaspoons vanilla extract
1½ cups coarsely chopped toasted
    pecans (see Note)
1 cup toffee pieces

NOTE: To toast the pecans, place on a baking sheet in a 350-degree oven for 15 minutes, or until lightly browned and fragrant.

Preheat oven to 350 degrees.

In a small bowl, combine the flour, baking soda, and salt. Set aside.

In a large bowl, cream the butter with the sugars until smooth, about 2 minutes. Add the egg and vanilla, and beat well. Add the dry ingredients and mix thoroughly. Stir in the pecans and toffee. Drop by rounded teaspoonfuls onto ungreased cookie sheets, leaving several inches between for expansion. Bake for 10–12 minutes, or until lightly golden.

Cool the cookies on the sheets for 5 minutes, and then remove to a wire rack to cool completely.

MAKES 4 DOZEN COOKIES

Almond Crescent Cookies

Jennifer sampled this simple and scrumptious cookie at a Christmas party. She was so delighted by it that the hostess gave her the recipe, which came from her grandmother.

1 cup (2 sticks) unsalted butter, softened
⅓ cup sugar
1 teaspoon vanilla extract

¼ teaspoon almond extract
1 cup finely ground almonds
2¼ cups all-purpose flour
Confectioners' sugar for sprinkling

Preheat oven to 350 degrees.

In a large bowl, cream the butter and the sugar until fluffy, about 3 minutes. Add the vanilla extract, the almond extract, and the ground almonds and mix until all the ingredients are thoroughly incorporated. Slowly mix in the flour. Make a ball with the dough and roll small pieces of the dough into ovals, then form crescents. Place onto ungreased cookie sheets, leaving several inches between for expansion. Bake 12–15 minutes until lightly browned.

Cool the cookies on the sheet for 1 minute, then remove to a rack to cool completely. When cooled, sprinkle with confectioners' sugar.

MAKES ABOUT 4½ DOZEN COOKIES

Peanut Butter Cup Cookies

Peanut butter cups, peanut butter chips, and peanuts—need we say more?

2¼ cups all-purpose flour
1 teaspoon baking soda
½ teaspoon salt
1 cup (2 sticks) unsalted butter, softened
½ cup sugar
½ cup firmly packed light brown sugar

1 large egg, at room temperature
1½ teaspoons vanilla extract
1½ cups coarsely chopped, chilled peanut butter cups (9–10 pieces)
¾ cup peanut butter chips
½ cup finely chopped unsalted peanuts

Preheat oven to 350 degrees.

In a large bowl, combine the flour, the baking soda, and the salt. Set aside.

In a large bowl, cream the butter and the sugars until smooth, about 3 minutes. Add the egg and mix well. Add the vanilla. Add the flour mixture and beat thoroughly. Stir in the peanut butter cups, the peanut butter chips, and the peanuts. Drop by rounded teaspoonfuls onto ungreased cookie sheets, leaving several inches between for expansion. Bake for 10–12 minutes or until lightly browned.

Cool the cookies on the sheets for 1 minute, then remove to a rack to cool completely.

MAKES ABOUT 3½ DOZEN COOKIES

Chocolate Chocolate Chip Drop Cookies

An old-fashioned, chewy chocolate cookie with little extra bursts of chocolate from the miniature chips.

1 cup all-purpose flour
6 tablespoons unsweetened
   Dutch process cocoa
½ teaspoon baking powder
¼ teaspoon salt
5 tablespoons unsalted butter,
   softened
5 tablespoons solid vegetable
   shortening

1 cup sugar plus 1 tablespoon
   (for sprinkling)
1 large egg, at room temperature
1 teaspoon vanilla extract
½ cup miniature semisweet chocolate
   chips

In a small bowl, combine the flour, cocoa, baking powder, and salt. Set aside.

In a large bowl, cream the butter, shortening, and sugar until smooth, about 3 minutes. Add the egg and vanilla, and beat well. Add the dry ingredients and mix thoroughly. Stir in the chocolate chips. Drop by rounded teaspoonfuls onto ungreased cookie sheets, leaving several inches between for expansion. Sprinkle lightly with the sugar. Place the cookie sheets in the refrigerator and chill for 20 minutes.

Preheat oven to 350 degrees.

Bake for 10–12 minutes. Cool the cookies on the sheets for 5 minutes and then remove to a wire rack to cool completely.

MAKES 2 DOZEN COOKIES

Raspberry Hazelnut Linzer Cookies

These cookies were another big Christmastime favorite at the bakery. They require a few steps but are really not difficult to make and are quite festive.

3 cups all-purpose flour
¼ teaspoon salt
1½ cups (3 sticks) unsalted butter, softened
1 cup sugar
1½ teaspoons vanilla extract

1 cup finely chopped (not ground) toasted hazelnuts (see Note)
⅓ cup raspberry preserves
½ cup confectioners' sugar (for dredging)

NOTE: To toast the hazelnuts, place on a baking sheet in a 350-degree oven for 15 minutes, or until lightly browned and fragrant.

In a small bowl, combine the flour and salt. Set aside.

In a large bowl, cream the butter and sugar until smooth, about two minutes. Add the vanilla and beat well. Add the dry ingredients in three parts, adding the nuts with the last portion, and mix until just combined. Shape the dough into two flat disks, wrap each disk tightly with plastic wrap, and refrigerate for 30 minutes.

Working with one disk at a time, roll out the dough on a lightly floured surface to ¼-inch thickness. Using a 3-inch fluted cutter, cut out the cookies and place them on baking sheets lined with waxed paper. Place the baking sheets in the refrigerator and chill for an additional 15 minutes.

Preheat oven to 350 degrees.

Remove the baking sheets from the refrigerator, and using a ½-inch fluted cutter, cut a circle out of the center of half of the cookies. Arrange on ungreased baking sheets, 2 inches apart, and bake for 15–18 minutes, or until lightly golden around the edges.

Cool the cookies on the sheets for 5 minutes, and then remove to a wire rack to cool completely.

Spread 1 teaspoon of preserves on the flat side of the cookies without the cutout centers. Sandwich the cutout cookies with the cookies spread with the preserves. Dredge the cookies on both sides with the confectioners' sugar.

MAKES 20 COOKIES

Orange Vanilla Chip Cookies

These cookies were inspired by a recipe in *Country Living* magazine. It's rather unique and reminds us of eating Creamsicles. People's mouths water over these! If you can't find vanilla chips, use white chocolate chips.

2¼ cups all-purpose flour
¾ teaspoon baking soda
½ teaspoon salt
1 cup (2 sticks) unsalted butter, softened

½ cup sugar
½ cup firmly packed light brown sugar
1 large egg, at room temperature
1 tablespoon grated orange zest
1 cup vanilla chips

Preheat oven to 350 degrees.

In a large bowl, sift together the flour, the baking soda, and the salt. Set aside.

In a large bowl, cream the butter with the sugars until smooth, about 3 minutes. Add the egg and mix well. Add the flour mixture and beat thoroughly. Stir in the orange zest and the vanilla chips. Drop by rounded teaspoonfuls onto ungreased cookie sheets, leaving several inches between for expansion. Bake for 10–12 minutes or until lightly golden brown.

Cool the cookies on the sheets for 1 minute, then remove to a rack to cool completely.

MAKES 2–3 DOZEN COOKIES

White Chocolate Coconut Macadamia Cookies

All the exotic tastes of a tropical island wrapped up in one yummy cookie.

2½ cups all-purpose flour
1 teaspoon baking soda
½ teaspoon salt
1 cup (2 sticks) unsalted butter, softened
⅔ cup sugar
⅔ cup firmly packed light brown sugar
1 large egg, at room temperature

2 tablespoons milk
1½ teaspoons vanilla extract
6 ounces white chocolate, coarsely chopped
1 cup sweetened shredded coconut
1 cup coarsely chopped macadamia nuts

Preheat oven to 350 degrees.

In a large bowl, combine the flour, the baking soda, and the salt. Set aside.

In a large bowl, cream the butter and the sugars until smooth, about 3 minutes. Add the egg, the milk, and the vanilla and mix well. Add the dry ingredients and beat thoroughly. Stir in the white chocolate, the coconut, and the nuts. Drop by rounded teaspoons onto ungreased cookie sheets, leaving several inches between for expansion. Bake for 10–12 minutes or until lightly golden.

Cool the cookies on the sheets for 1 minute, then remove to a rack to cool completely.

MAKES ABOUT 3 DOZEN COOKIES

Iced Ginger Cookies

Allysa's been making these cookies for years now, and still gets really excited every autumn when she bakes the first batch of the season. They're chewy and spicy with just the right amount of sweet icing.

COOKIE
2 cups all-purpose flour
2 teaspoons baking soda
1 teaspoon ginger
1 teaspoon cinnamon
½ teaspoon salt
¾ cup vegetable oil (preferably canola)
1 cup sugar plus 1 tablespoon
    (for sprinkling)

1 large egg, at room temperature
¼ cup light unsulphured molasses

ICING
½ cup confectioners' sugar, sifted
1 tablespoon solid vegetable
    shortening
2 teaspoons water

Preheat oven to 350 degrees.

In a small bowl, combine the flour, baking soda, ginger, cinnamon, and salt. Set aside.

In a large bowl, on the medium speed of an electric mixer, beat together the oil and sugar for 2–3 minutes. Add the egg and molasses, and beat well. Add the dry ingredients and mix thoroughly. Drop by rounded teaspoonfuls onto ungreased cookie sheets, leaving several inches between for expansion. Sprinkle lightly with sugar. Bake for 12 minutes. Cool the cookies on the sheets for 5 minutes, and then remove to a wire rack to cool completely.

To make the icing: Combine the sugar, shortening, and water, and beat until smooth and creamy. Cover until ready to use.

When the cookies are completely cool, spread a very thin layer of icing on each cookie with a small knife or spatula. Let the icing set before stacking the cookies or they will stick together.

MAKES 2½ DOZEN COOKIES

Peanut Butter Cookies

This recipe has evolved over many years of experimentation. We think that we have discovered the secret to the perfect peanut butter cookie.

1 ¼ cups all-purpose flour
¾ teaspoon baking soda
½ teaspoon baking powder
¼ teaspoon salt
½ cup (1 stick) unsalted butter, softened
1 cup chunky-style peanut butter, at room temperature

¾ cup sugar plus 1 tablespoon (for sprinkling)
½ cup firmly packed light brown sugar
1 large egg, at room temperature
1 tablespoon milk
1 teaspoon vanilla extract
1 cup peanut butter chips

Preheat oven to 350 degrees.

In a large bowl, combine the flour, the baking soda, the baking powder, and the salt. Set aside.

In a large bowl, beat the butter and the peanut butter together until fluffy. Add the sugars and beat until smooth. Add the egg and mix well. Add the milk and the vanilla. Add the flour mixture and beat thoroughly. Stir in the peanut butter chips. Drop by rounded teaspoonfuls onto ungreased cookie sheets, leaving several inches between for expansion. Using a fork, lightly indent with a crisscross pattern, but do not overly flatten cookies. Lightly sprinkle cookies with sugar. Bake for 10–12 minutes. Do not over-bake. Cookies may appear to be underdone, but they are not.

Cool the cookies on the sheets for 1 minute, then remove to a rack to cool completely.

MAKES 2–3 DOZEN COOKIES

White Chocolate Pecan Drop Cookies

Two of Allysa's favorite ingredients—toasted pecans and creamy white chocolate—together in what is definitely the most often baked cookie at her house.

1 ½ cups all-purpose flour

1 teaspoon baking soda

½ teaspoon salt

⅔ cup (1 ⅓ sticks) unsalted butter, softened

½ cup sugar

½ cup firmly packed light brown sugar

1 large egg, at room temperature

1 teaspoon vanilla extract

1 cup coarsely chopped toasted pecans (see Note)

⅔ cup coarsely chopped white chocolate (preferably Lindt)

NOTE: To toast the pecans, place on a baking sheet in a 350-degree oven for 15 minutes, or until lightly browned and fragrant.

Preheat oven to 350 degrees.

In a small bowl, combine the flour, baking soda, and salt. Set aside.

In a large bowl, cream the butter with the sugars until smooth, about two minutes. Add the egg and vanilla, and beat well. Add the dry ingredients and mix thoroughly. Stir in the pecans and white chocolate. Drop by rounded teaspoonfuls onto ungreased cookie sheets, leaving several inches between for expansion. Bake for 10–12 minutes, or until lightly golden.

Cool the cookies on the sheets for 5 minutes, and then remove to a wire rack to cool completely.

MAKES 3 DOZEN COOKIES

Snickerdoodles

This soft cinnamon-sugar cookie has been around for ages, and who knows where the name comes from! When Allysa was growing up, she always made them at Christmastime.

2½ cups all-purpose flour
2 teaspoons cream of tartar
1 teaspoon baking soda
¼ teaspoon salt
1 cup (2 sticks) unsalted butter, softened

1½ cups sugar
2 large eggs, at room temperature
2 tablespoons milk
1 teaspoon vanilla extract
6 tablespoons sugar mixed with
      2 teaspoons cinnamon, for sprinkling

In a small bowl, combine the flour, cream of tartar, baking soda, and salt. Set aside.

In a large bowl, cream the butter and sugar until smooth, about 2 minutes. Add the eggs, milk, and vanilla, and beat well. Add the dry ingredients and mix thoroughly. Wrap the dough tightly with plastic wrap and chill in the refrigerator for 2 hours.

Preheat oven to 350 degrees.

Drop by rounded teaspoonfuls onto ungreased cookie sheets, leaving several inches between for expansion. (I recommend leaving extra room between these cookies because they spread more than most.) Sprinkle generously with the cinnamon-sugar mixture. Bake for 12–14 minutes.

Cool the cookies on the sheets for 5 minutes, and then remove to a wire rack to cool completely.

MAKES 3 DOZEN COOKIES

Iced Molasses Cookies

Gingerbread fans will adore this cookie. We sweetened them just a bit with some tasty sugar icing.

COOKIE
2 cups all-purpose flour, sifted
2 teaspoons baking soda
½ teaspoon salt
1 tablespoon allspice
1 teaspoon cinnamon
¾ cup (1 ½ sticks) unsalted butter, softened
¾ cup sugar

1 large egg
¼ cup light, unsulphured molasses

ICING
4 tablespoons solid vegetable shortening
2 cups confectioners' sugar
2–3 tablespoons water

Preheat oven to 350 degrees.

In a large bowl, combine the already sifted flour with the other dry ingredients and sift again. Set aside.

In a large bowl, cream the butter and the sugar until smooth, about 3 minutes. Add the egg and mix well. Beat in the molasses. Add the dry ingredients and mix thoroughly. Drop by rounded teaspoonfuls onto ungreased cookie sheets, leaving several inches between for expansion. Bake for 10–12 minutes.

Cool the cookies on the sheets for 1 minute, then remove to a rack to cool completely.

To make the icing, combine the shortening, the sugar, and the water and beat until smooth. Cover until ready to use.

When cookies are completely cool, spread a thin layer of icing on each cookie with a small knife or spatula. Let icing set before stacking cookies, or they will stick together.

MAKES 3–4 DOZEN COOKIES

Peanut Butter Chocolate Chip Pecan Cookies

For those of you who can't resist adding peanut butter to desserts, this is basically a chocolate chip cookie with peanut butter chips as well. The milk in the batter gives these cookies a lovely texture.

2 ½ cups all-purpose flour
1 teaspoon baking soda
½ teaspoon salt
1 cup (2 sticks) unsalted butter, softened
1 cup firmly packed light brown sugar
⅓ cup sugar

1 large egg, at room temperature
2 tablespoons milk
1 ½ teaspoons vanilla extract
1 ½ cups coarsely chopped toasted pecans (see Note)
1 cup peanut butter chips
½ cup semisweet chocolate chips

NOTE: To toast the pecans, place on a baking sheet in a 350-degree oven for 15 minutes, or until lightly browned and fragrant.

Preheat oven to 350 degrees.

In a small bowl, combine the flour, baking soda, and salt. Set aside.

In a large bowl, cream the butter with sugars until smooth, about 2 minutes. Add the egg, milk, and vanilla, and beat well. Add the dry ingredients and mix thoroughly. Stir in the pecans, peanut butter chips, and chocolate chips. Drop by rounded teaspoonfuls onto ungreased cookie sheets, leaving several inches between for expansion. Bake for 10–12 minutes, or until lightly golden.

Cool the cookies on the sheets for 5 minutes, and then remove to a wire rack to cool completely.

MAKES 5 DOZEN COOKIES

Coconut Oatmeal Drop Cookies

Allysa is always striving to make the perfect crispy but chewy oatmeal cookie. She's not fond of raisins, so she adds coconut instead for extra texture and sweetness.

1 ½ cups all-purpose flour
1 teaspoon baking soda
1 teaspoon cinnamon
¼ teaspoon salt
1 cup (2 sticks) unsalted butter, softened
1 cup firmly packed light brown sugar

½ cup sugar
1 large egg, at room temperature
1 ½ teaspoons vanilla extract
1 ½ cups rolled oats (not quick-cooking)
1 cup sweetened shredded coconut

Preheat oven to 375 degrees.

In a small bowl, combine the flour, baking soda, cinnamon, and salt. Set aside.

In a large bowl, cream the butter with the sugars until smooth, about 2 minutes. Add the egg and vanilla, and beat well. Add the dry ingredients and mix thoroughly. Stir in the oats and coconut. Drop by rounded teaspoonfuls onto ungreased cookie sheets, leaving several inches between for expansion. Bake for 12–14 minutes, or until lightly golden.

Cool the cookies on the sheets for 5 minutes, and then remove to a wire rack to cool completely.

MAKES 3½ DOZEN COOKIES

BROWNIES
AND
BAR COOKIES

White Chocolate Pecan Bars

This bar cookie has a really nice brown sugar shortbread base with a topping of white chocolate and pecans.

BAR

2 cups all-purpose flour

½ teaspoon salt

1 cup (2 sticks) unsalted butter, softened

1 cup firmly packed light brown sugar

1 large egg, at room temperature

1 teaspoon vanilla extract

½ cup coarsely chopped toasted pecans (see Note)

TOPPING

1 ½ cups coarsely chopped white chocolate

½ cup coarsely chopped toasted pecans (see Note)

NOTE: To toast the pecans, place on a baking sheet in a 350-degree oven for 15 minutes, or until lightly browned and fragrant.

Preheat oven to 350 degrees.

Grease and lightly flour a 13 x 9-inch baking pan.

In a small bowl, combine the flour and salt. Set aside.

In a large bowl, beat together the butter, sugar, egg, and vanilla until creamy, about 2–3 minutes. Add the dry ingredients and mix thoroughly. Stir in the pecans. Spread the batter evenly in the prepared pan. Bake for 25 minutes.

Remove from the oven and immediately sprinkle the white chocolate on top. Let stand for 5 minutes and then gently spread the melted chocolate in a thin layer over the bars. Sprinkle with the pecans.

Allow to cool to room temperature (the white chocolate should harden) or overnight before cutting and serving.

MAKES TWENTY-FOUR 2-INCH BARS

Fudge Brownies with White Chocolate, Toffee, and Pecans

Quite possibly the richest and darkest chocolate brownie you'll ever taste. The mother of one of our employees used to forgo her diet every time she visited Magnolia to have one of these. Don't worry, Mrs. W., we're sure you're not alone!

BROWNIE
1 cup all-purpose flour
1 ½ teaspoons baking powder
¾ teaspoon salt
12 ounces unsweetened chocolate
1 cup (2 sticks) unsalted butter
3 cups sugar
6 large eggs, at room temperature

2 tablespoons vanilla
    extract

TOPPING
¾ cup toffee pieces
¾ cup finely chopped pecans
1 ½ cups white chocolate, coarsely
    chopped

Preheat oven to 350 degrees.

Grease a 12 x 18-inch jelly roll pan.

To make the brownie: In a large bowl, sift together the flour, the baking powder, and the salt. Set aside.

In a medium-size saucepan over low heat, melt the chocolate with the butter, stirring occasionally until smooth. Cool for 5–10 minutes. Transfer this mixture to a large bowl and mix in the sugar, the eggs, and the vanilla. Add the dry ingredients. Pour the batter into prepared pan. Sprinkle the toffee and the pecans evenly over the batter. Bake 25–28 minutes or until a cake tester inserted into center of pan comes out with moist crumbs attached. Do not overbake.

Let cool for 20 minutes, then sprinkle the white chocolate chunks over the brownies.

Allow to cool to room temperature, or overnight, before cutting and serving.

MAKES TWENTY-FOUR 3-INCH BROWNIES

Apple Walnut Cake
with Caramel Cream Cheese Icing

Caramel Pecan Brownies; Fudge Brownies with White Chocolate, Toffee, and Pecans; Peanut Butter Fudge Brownies; Raspberry Crumb Squares

Lemon Icebox Pie

Oatmeal, Blueberry, and Corn Muffins

Aunt Daisy's Fresh Fruit Torte

Traditional Vanilla Birthday Cake cupcake
with Traditional Vanilla Buttercream

Poppy Seed Coffee Cake

Coconut Layer Cake and Devil's Food Cake
with Chocolate Buttercream

Strawberry Oat Bars

This versatile bar is equally delicious as a breakfast bar or a mid-afternoon pick-me-up. It goes great with a hot cup of apple cider.

CRUST

2½ cups (5 sticks) unsalted butter, melted

4¼ cups all-purpose flour

1½ cups rolled oats (not quick-cooking oats)

¾ cup confectioners' sugar

FILLING

1 twenty-one-ounce can strawberry pie filling

TOPPING

1¾ cups all-purpose flour

½ cup brown sugar

1¼ cups rolled oats

1½ cups confectioners' sugar

½ teaspoon cinnamon

½ cup chopped toasted almonds (see Note)

1 cup (2 sticks) unsalted butter, softened, cut into small pieces

NOTE: To toast almonds, place on a baking sheet in a 325-degree oven for approximately 10–15 minutes or until lightly browned and fragrant.

Preheat oven to 350 degrees.

To make the crust: In a large bowl, combine the butter, the flour, the oats, and the sugar, forming a doughlike consistency.

Spread crust evenly into an ungreased 12 x 18-inch jelly roll pan. Use a large piece of waxed paper to firmly and evenly press down crust. Bake the crust for 16–18 minutes. Remove from oven and let cool for 15–20 minutes.

While the crust is cooling, prepare the topping: In a large bowl, mix together the first six ingredients. Using a pastry blender, cut in the butter until the mixture resembles coarse crumbs.

When the crust is cool, gently and evenly spread the strawberry filling over the crust, leaving a ¼-inch edge all around. Sprinkle crumbs generously, allowing the filling to peek through. Bake for an additional 10–12 minutes until lightly golden.

Allow to cool to room temperature, or overnight, before cutting and serving.

MAKES TWENTY-FOUR 3-INCH BARS

Vanilla Pecan Brownies

This fabulous square is a double treat for vanilla lovers, with vanilla chips melted in and plenty sprinkled on top. The pecans lend a delightful crunch.

BROWNIE

1 ⅓ cups (2 ⅔ sticks) unsalted butter, melted
2 cups vanilla chips
6 large eggs
1 ⅓ cups sugar
1 tablespoon vanilla extract

2 ⅔ cups all-purpose flour
½ teaspoon salt

TOPPING

1 cup vanilla chips
¾ cup chopped pecans

Preheat oven to 350 degrees.

Grease a 12 x 18-inch jelly roll pan.

In a medium-size saucepan, melt the butter with 2 cups of the vanilla chips over low heat, stirring often. Remove from heat and cool for 5–10 minutes.

In a large bowl, on the low speed of an electric mixer, beat the eggs until light and creamy, about 3 minutes. Gradually add the sugar. Beat in the vanilla chip mixture. Add the vanilla and beat until smooth.

Add the flour and the salt, beating until well combined. Pour the batter into prepared pan. Sprinkle additional 1 cup vanilla chips and ¾ cup pecans evenly over brownie batter.

Bake for 18–22 minutes or until a cake tester inserted into center of pan comes out with moist crumbs attached.

Allow to cool to room temperature, or overnight, before cutting and serving.

MAKES TWENTY-FOUR 3-INCH BROWNIES

Apple Bars with Oatmeal Crumb Topping

A perfect autumn treat—all the flavors of apple pie, but unlike the more fragile pie, these bars are easily wrapped up for lunches and picnics.

CRUST
1 cup (2 sticks) unsalted butter, softened and cut into small pieces
2 cups all-purpose flour

TOPPING
1½ cups all-purpose flour
1 cup firmly packed light brown sugar
⅔ cup rolled oats (not quick-cooking) plus 3 tablespoons (for sprinkling)

½ teaspoon cinnamon
⅔ cup (1⅓ sticks) unsalted butter, softened and cut into small pieces

FILLING
One 21-ounce can apple pie filling

GLAZE
1 cup confectioners' sugar, sifted
1 tablespoon plus 1 teaspoon water

Preheat oven to 350 degrees.

To make the crust: In a large bowl, on the medium speed of an electric mixer, beat together the butter and flour until crumbly and well combined. Transfer the mixture to an ungreased 13 x 9-inch baking pan and, using your hands, pat the crust firmly and evenly into the pan. Bake for 20 minutes. Remove from the oven and allow to cool completely, about 45 minutes.

To make the topping: In a large bowl, mix together the flour, sugar, oats, and cinnamon. Using a pastry blender, cut in the butter until the mixture resembles coarse crumbs. Then, using your hands, toss until all the ingredients are well combined. Set aside.

When the crust is cool, gently and evenly spread the apple filling over the crust, leaving a ¼-inch edge all around. Sprinkle the crumb topping over the filling, then sprinkle the additional 3 tablespoons of rolled oats over the crumb topping. Bake for 45 minutes. Allow to cool to room temperature.

To make the glaze: Combine the sugar and water, and beat until smooth. Cover until ready to use. When the bars are completely cool, drizzle the glaze decoratively over the crumb topping. Allow the glaze to set for 15–20 minutes before cutting and serving.

MAKES TWENTY-FOUR 2-INCH BARS

Magic Cookie Bars

In Texas a variation of these bars are called Hello Dollys (see that recipe on p. 86). No matter what you call them, they're a huge childhood favorite whose popularity "will never go away again"!

4½ cups graham cracker crumbs
1½ cups (3 sticks) unsalted butter, melted
2 cups chopped walnuts

1 cup miniature chocolate chips
4½ cups sweetened, shredded coconut
3 fourteen-ounce cans sweetened condensed milk

Preheat oven to 325 degrees.

To make the crust: In a large bowl, combine the graham cracker crumbs with the melted butter. Press firmly into an ungreased 12 x 18-inch jelly roll pan.

Sprinkle over this the walnuts, then the chocolate chips, and then the coconut. On top, pour over three cans of sweetened condensed milk evenly, to completely cover the coconut. Use a spatula to spread if necessary.

Bake for 30–35 minutes or until lightly golden. Do not overbake.

Allow to cool to room temperature, or overnight, before cutting and serving.

MAKES TWENTY-FOUR 3-INCH BARS

Raspberry Crunch Squares

This scrumptious bar is a perfect blend of fruit and crumb. Serve it with a dollop of whipped cream if you like. You can try any of your favorite preserves as a filling; you can't go wrong!

CRUST

2 cups (4 sticks) unsalted butter, melted

4 cups all-purpose flour

FILLING

1 ¼ cups raspberry preserves (beaten smooth with a mixer or a spoon)

TOPPING

4 ½ cups all-purpose flour

3 cups unpacked light brown sugar

2 cups (4 sticks) unsalted butter, softened, cut into small pieces

Preheat oven to 350 degrees.

To make the crust: In a large bowl, combine the butter with the flour until you get a doughlike consistency.

Spread crust evenly into an ungreased 12 x 18-inch jelly roll pan. Use a large piece of waxed paper to firmly and evenly press down crust. Bake the crust for 15 minutes. Remove from oven and let cool completely, 30–40 minutes.

While the crust is cooling, prepare the topping: Mix the flour and the brown sugar. Using a pastry blender, cut in the butter until the mixture resembles coarse crumbs.

When the crust is cool, gently and evenly spread the raspberry preserves over the crust, leaving a ¼-inch edge all around. Sprinkle crumbs generously over the preserves (it will seem like more than you think you need).

Bake for an additional 15–18 minutes until golden brown.

Allow to cool to room temperature, or overnight, before cutting and serving.

MAKES TWENTY-FOUR 3-INCH SQUARES

Apricot Cream Cheese Streusel Bars

This delicate bar combines a creamy filling with apricot preserves and a sweet crumb topping.

CRUST
1 cup (2 sticks) unsalted butter,
    softened and cut into small pieces
2 cups all-purpose flour

CREAM CHEESE FILLING
½ pound (one 8-ounce package)
    cream cheese (not softened)
⅓ cup sugar
1 large egg, at room temperature
1 teaspoon vanilla extract

STREUSEL TOPPING
1 ½ cups all-purpose flour
1 ½ cups confectioners' sugar
¾ cup (1 ½ sticks) unsalted butter,
    softened and cut into small pieces

APRICOT FILLING
¾ cup apricot preserves (preferably
    unsweetened)

Preheat oven to 350 degrees.

To make the crust: In a large bowl, on the medium speed of an electric mixer, beat together the butter and flour until crumbly and well combined. Transfer the mixture to an ungreased 13 x 9-inch baking pan and, using your hands, pat the crust firmly and evenly into the pan. Bake for 15 minutes. Remove from the oven and allow to cool completely, about 45 minutes.

To make the cream cheese filling: In a medium-size bowl, on the medium speed of an electric mixer, beat together the cream cheese and sugar until smooth and creamy. Add the egg and vanilla, and continue to beat until well combined. Set aside.

To make the streusel topping: In a medium-size bowl, mix together the flour and sugar. Using a pastry blender, cut in the butter until the mixture resembles coarse crumbs. Then, using your hands, toss until the ingredients are well combined. Set aside.

When the crust is cool, spread the cream cheese filling evenly over the crust, leaving a ¼-inch edge all around. Gently spread a thin layer of apricot filling over the cream cheese. Sprinkle the streusel topping over the entire top. Bake for 35 minutes. Cool to room temperature, cover tightly with plastic wrap, and allow to set overnight before cutting and serving.

MAKES TWENTY-FOUR 2-INCH BARS

Caramel Pecan Brownies

These cakelike brownies combine a graham cracker crust and crunchy caramel topping to taste almost like candy. You'll be tempted to lick your fingers. Go ahead—we won't tell!

CRUST
4½ cups graham cracker crumbs
1½ cups (3 sticks) unsalted butter, melted

BROWNIE
2⅔ cups all-purpose flour
2 teaspoons baking powder
1 teaspoon salt
8 ounces unsweetened chocolate

1⅓ cups (2⅔ sticks) unsalted butter
8 large eggs, at room temperature
4 cups sugar
4 teaspoons vanilla extract

TOPPING
1½ cups coarsely chopped pecans
¾ cup cold Caramel Sauce (see recipe on page 140)

Preheat oven to 350 degrees.

To make the crust: In a medium-size bowl, combine the graham cracker crumbs with the melted butter. Press firmly into an ungreased 12 x 18-inch jelly roll pan.

To make the brownie: In a large bowl, sift together the flour, the baking powder, and the salt. Set aside.

In a medium-size saucepan over low heat, melt the chocolate and the butter, stirring occasionally until smooth. Remove from heat and cool for 5–10 minutes.

Meanwhile, beat the eggs until light and creamy, about 2–3 minutes. Gradually add the sugar. Add the chocolate mixture and mix well. Add the sifted dry ingredients, beating until well combined. Add the vanilla. Pour the batter into prepared crust. Sprinkle the pecans over the batter. Bake 30–35 minutes or until a cake tester inserted into center of pan comes out with moist crumbs attached. Do not overbake.

When completely cooled, drizzle caramel over brownies.

MAKES TWENTY-FOUR 3-INCH BROWNIES

Pumpkin Bars with Cream Cheese Icing

We used to start making these bars at the bakery the week of Halloween. And every year both the customers and the staff could hardly wait that long. They're very, very good.

BARS
1 ½ cups all-purpose flour
1 ½ teaspoons baking powder
1 ½ teaspoons cinnamon
1 teaspoon baking soda
¼ teaspoon salt
1 ¼ cups canned pumpkin puree
1 ¼ cups sugar
¾ cup vegetable oil (preferably canola)
3 large eggs, at room temperature

½ cup coarsely chopped toasted pecans (see Note)

ICING
½ recipe Cream Cheese Icing (page 128)

GARNISH
½ cup coarsely chopped toasted pecans (see Note)

NOTE: To toast the pecans, place on a baking sheet in a 350-degree oven for 15 minutes, or until lightly browned and fragrant.

Preheat oven to 350 degrees.

Grease and lightly flour a 13 x 9-inch baking pan.

To make the bars: In a small bowl, sift together the flour, baking powder, cinnamon, baking soda, and salt. Set aside.

In a large bowl, on the medium speed of an electric mixer, beat together the pumpkin, sugar, oil, and eggs until smooth, about 3 minutes. Add the dry ingredients and mix thoroughly. Stir in the pecans. Pour the batter into the prepared pan. Bake for 25–30 minutes, or until a cake tester inserted in the center of the pan comes out clean.

Remove from the oven and allow to cool completely before icing the top with the cream cheese icing. Garnish with pecans as desired.

MAKES TWELVE 3-INCH BARS

Shelly's Cherry Squares

This recipe comes from Shelly Sinko, who baked at Magnolia for many years. It's based on a cookie that her mom made when she was growing up.

½ cup (1 stick) unsalted butter, softened
1 ½ cups sugar
4 large eggs, at room temperature
1 teaspoon vanilla extract
2 cups all-purpose flour
½ cup canned cherry pie filling
Confectioners' sugar for sprinkling

Preheat oven to 350 degrees.

Grease and lightly flour a 13 x 9-inch baking pan.

In a large bowl, on the medium speed of an electric mixer, cream the butter with the sugar until smooth, about 2 minutes. Add the eggs, one at a time, beating well after each addition. Add the vanilla. Add the flour and mix thoroughly.

Spread the dough evenly in the prepared pan. With a small, sharp knife, score into twenty-four 2-inch squares.

Place a teaspoon of cherry pie filling (each containing one cherry) on each scored square. Bake for 30–35 minutes, or until a cake tester inserted in the center of the pan comes out clean.

Allow to cool to room temperature, then sprinkle generously with confectioners' sugar before cutting and serving.

MAKES TWENTY-FOUR 2-INCH SQUARES

Blondies with Cream Cheese Swirl and Pecans

There have been lots of recipes over the years for cream cheese swirl brownies, but never the blondie and cream cheese combination, which seemed perfect. If you are not a huge chocolate fan, you'll love these.

CREAM CHEESE FILLING

4 ounces (one-half of an 8-ounce package) cream cheese (not softened)

2 tablespoons sugar

1 large egg yolk, at room temperature

1 tablespoon all-purpose flour

BLONDIES

1 ½ cups cake flour (not self-rising)

1 teaspoon baking powder

¼ teaspoon salt

¾ cup (1 ½ sticks) unsalted butter, softened

1 ¼ cups firmly packed light brown sugar

¼ cup sugar

2 large eggs, at room temperature

2 teaspoons vanilla extract

½ cup coarsely chopped toasted pecans (see Note)

NOTE: To toast the pecans, place on a baking sheet in a 350-degree oven for 15 minutes, or until lightly browned and fragrant.

Preheat oven to 350 degrees.

Grease and lightly flour a 13 x 9-inch baking pan.

To make the cream cheese filling: In a medium-size bowl, beat the cream cheese and sugar until smooth. Add the egg yolk and flour, and beat well. Set aside.

To make the blondies: In a small bowl, combine the flour, baking powder, and salt. Set aside. In a large bowl, cream the butter with the sugars until smooth, about 2 minutes. Add the eggs and vanilla, and beat well. Add the dry ingredients and mix thoroughly. Spread the batter evenly in the prepared pan.

Drop the cream cheese mixture by teaspoonfuls over the batter. Using a small knife, swirl the cream cheese into the batter, forming a decorative pattern. Sprinkle the pecans evenly over the batter.

Bake for 35–40 minutes, or until a cake tester inserted in the center of the pan comes out with moist crumbs attached. Do not overbake. Allow to cool to room temperature or overnight before cutting and serving.

MAKES TWENTY-FOUR 2-INCH BLONDIES

Coconut Pecan Shortbread Squares

This bar cookie has a simple shortbread crust and layers of pecans and coconut. It couldn't be easier to make—or more delicious.

CRUST
1 cup (2 sticks) unsalted butter, softened and cut into small pieces
2 cups all-purpose flour

TOPPING
2 cups coarsely chopped toasted pecans (see Note)

1 cup sweetened shredded coconut
One 14-ounce can sweetened condensed milk

NOTE: To toast the pecans, place on a baking sheet in a 350-degree oven for 15 minutes, or until lightly browned and fragrant.

Preheat oven to 350 degrees.

To make the crust: In a large bowl, on the medium speed of an electric mixer, beat together the butter and flour until crumbly and well combined. Transfer the mixture to an ungreased 13 x 9-inch baking pan and, using your hands, pat the crust firmly and evenly into the pan. Bake for 15 minutes. Remove from the oven and allow to cool for 30 minutes.

Sprinkle the pecans and then the coconut over the crust. Pour the can of sweetened condensed milk on top to completely cover the coconut. Use a spatula to spread it if necessary. Bake for 30–35 minutes, or until lightly golden.

Cool to room temperature, cover tightly with plastic wrap, and allow to set overnight before cutting and serving.

MAKES TWENTY-FOUR 2-INCH SQUARES

Butterscotch Cream Cheese Swirl Brownies

Here's a unique brownie for butterscotch fans. The cream cheese balances out the sweetness of the butterscotch nicely. Your mouth will be watering in no time!

CREAM CHEESE FILLING

8 ounces (1 package) cream cheese, softened
¼ cup sugar
1 large egg, at room temperature
2 tablespoons all-purpose flour

BROWNIE

2 cups all-purpose flour
2 teaspoons baking powder

½ teaspoon salt
2 cups butterscotch chips
½ cup (1 stick) unsalted butter
2 cups firmly packed light brown sugar
4 large eggs, at room temperature
1 teaspoon vanilla extract
1 cup coarsely chopped walnuts

Preheat oven to 350 degrees.

Grease and flour a 12 x 18-inch jelly roll pan.

To prepare the cream cheese filling: In a medium-size bowl, beat the cream cheese and the sugar until smooth. Add the egg and beat well. Add the flour and beat until incorporated. Set aside.

To make the brownie: In a large bowl, sift together the flour, the baking powder, and the salt. Set aside.

In a medium-size saucepan over low heat, melt the butterscotch chips and the butter, stirring occasionally until smooth. Remove from heat and beat in the brown sugar until well blended. Allow to cool for 5 minutes.

Beat the eggs one at a time into the butterscotch mixture. Add the vanilla. Add the dry ingredients, beating until well combined. Stir in the walnuts. Pour the batter into prepared pan.

Drop the cream cheese mixture by teaspoonfuls over the batter. Using a small knife, swirl the cream cheese into the batter, forming a decorative pattern. Bake for 25–30 minutes or until a cake tester inserted into center of pan comes out with moist crumbs attached. Do not overbake.

Allow to cool to room temperature, or overnight, before cutting and serving.

MAKES TWENTY-FOUR 3-INCH BROWNIES

Peanut Butter Heath Bar Blondies

While experimenting with recipes for the first Magnolia cookbook, Allysa developed this variation on the traditional blondie. If you're a peanut butter lover, you'll be crazy about these!

BLONDIES

1 ½ cups (3 sticks) unsalted butter, softened
1 ½ cups smooth peanut butter
2 ½ cups sugar
3 large eggs, at room temperature
2 tablespoons vanilla extract
3 cups self-rising flour

TOPPING

1 cup peanut butter chips
3 tablespoons heavy cream
4 coarsely chopped Heath Bars or chocolate-covered toffee bars (about 1 cup)
½ cup finely chopped unsalted peanuts

Preheat oven to 325 degrees.

Grease and flour a 12 x 18-inch jelly roll pan.

In a large bowl, beat together the butter and the peanut butter until fluffy. Add the sugar and beat until smooth. Add the eggs and the vanilla and mix well. Add the flour and beat until well incorporated. Spread the batter evenly into prepared pan. Bake for 25–30 minutes or until a cake tester inserted into center of pan comes out with moist crumbs attached. Cool to room temperature.

To prepare the topping: In a small saucepan over medium heat, melt the peanut butter chips and the cream, stirring until smooth. Drizzle the peanut butter mixture decoratively over the cooled blondies. Sprinkle the Heath Bar pieces and the peanuts on top.

Allow to cool to room temperature, or overnight, before cutting and serving.

MAKES TWENTY-FOUR 3-INCH BLONDIES

Chocolate Fudge Brownies with Butterscotch Chips and Pecans

These are really dense, really fudgy brownies. Allysa's always loved the combination of butterscotch and chocolate.

½ cup all-purpose flour
⅛ teaspoon salt
4 tablespoons (½ stick) unsalted butter
8 ounces semisweet chocolate
2 ounces unsweetened chocolate

2 large eggs, at room temperature
1 cup sugar
2 teaspoons vanilla extract
1 cup coarsely chopped toasted pecans (see Note)
⅓ cup butterscotch chips

NOTE: To toast the pecans, place on a baking sheet in a 350-degree oven for 15 minutes, or until lightly browned and fragrant.

Preheat oven to 325 degrees.

Grease and lightly flour an 8 x 8-inch baking pan.

In a small bowl, combine the flour and salt. Set aside.

In a medium-size saucepan over low heat, melt the butter with the chocolates, stirring occasionally until smooth. Remove from the heat and allow to cool to lukewarm, 5–10 minutes.

Meanwhile, beat the eggs with the sugar until light and creamy, 2–3 minutes. Add the vanilla and beat well. Add the chocolate mixture and beat until well combined. Add the dry ingredients and mix thoroughly. Stir in half of the pecans and half of the butterscotch chips. Spread the batter evenly in the prepared pan. Bake for 20 minutes. Remove from the oven and sprinkle the remaining pecans and butterscotch chips evenly over the brownie batter. Return to the oven and bake for an additional 15–20 minutes, or until a cake tester inserted in the center of the pan comes out with moist crumbs attached. Do not overbake.

Allow to cool to room temperature or overnight before cutting and serving.

MAKES SIXTEEN 2-INCH BROWNIES

Lemon Bars

Jennifer formulated this recipe owing to the demand from our lemon-loving customers for a lemon bar.

CRUST
2 cups (4 sticks) unsalted butter, softened
4 cups all-purpose flour
1 cup confectioners' sugar
½ teaspoon salt
2 teaspoons grated lemon zest

TOPPING
2 cups sugar
6 large eggs, at room temperature
1 cup lemon juice
6 teaspoons grated lemon zest

Preheat oven to 350 degrees.

Grease a 12 x 18-inch jelly roll pan.

To make the crust: In a large bowl, on the low speed of an electric mixer, combine all the ingredients until mixture resembles coarse crumbs. Form the dough into a ball. Spread crust evenly into prepared pan. Use a large piece of waxed paper to firmly and evenly press down crust. Bake the crust for 18–20 minutes until lightly golden. Remove from oven and let cool for 15–20 minutes before proceeding.

While the crust is cooling, make the topping: In a medium-size bowl, on the low speed of an electric mixer, beat the sugar, the eggs, the lemon juice, and the zest until well combined. Pour over slightly warm crust. Return to oven. Bake 18–20 minutes until edges are golden brown. Remove from oven and let cool for about 20 minutes. Dust with confectioners' sugar.

Allow to cool to room temperature, or overnight, before cutting and serving.

MAKES TWENTY-FOUR 3-INCH BARS

Peanut Butter Fudge Brownies

Remember the old peanut butter versus chocolate argument? You don't have to decide—you can have an abundance of both in this unbelievable brownie!

CRUST
1 ¼ cups (2 ½ sticks) unsalted butter, melted
3 ⅓ cups all-purpose flour
⅔ cup confectioners' sugar
⅔ cup finely chopped peanuts
¼ teaspoon salt

PEANUT BUTTER FILLING
4 ounces (½ package) cream cheese, softened
⅔ cup smooth peanut butter
6 tablespoons sugar
1 egg
¼ cup milk

BROWNIE
1 cup all-purpose flour
1 teaspoon baking powder

½ teaspoon salt
½ cup (1 stick) unsalted butter, softened
2 cups sugar
4 large eggs, at room temperature
1 tablespoon plus 1 teaspoon vanilla extract
6 ounces unsweetened chocolate, melted (see Note)
½ cup peanut butter chips

GARNISH
¾ cup peanut butter chips

NOTE: To melt chocolate, place in a double boiler over simmering water on low heat for approximately 5–10 minutes. Stir occasionally until completely smooth and no pieces of chocolate remain. Remove from heat and let cool for 5–10 minutes.

Preheat oven to 350 degrees.

To make the crust: In a large bowl, combine all the ingredients. Form the dough into a ball and press firmly into an ungreased 12 x 18-inch jelly roll pan. Bake the crust for 10 minutes. Remove from oven and let cool for 15–20 minutes before proceeding.

Meanwhile, prepare the peanut butter filling: In a large bowl, on the low speed of an electric mixer, beat the cream cheese and the peanut butter until smooth. Beat in the sugar, the egg, and the milk until well incorporated. Set aside.

To make the brownie: In a medium-size bowl, sift together the flour, the baking powder, and the salt. Set aside.

In a large bowl, cream the butter and the sugar until fluffy, about 3 minutes. Add the eggs and the vanilla. Add the chocolate and mix until well incorporated. Add the dry ingredients. Stir in the peanut butter chips.

Reserve 1 cup of the brownie batter. Spread the rest of the brownie batter evenly over the cooled crust. Drop the peanut butter filling by large spoonfuls randomly over the entire surface of the brownie batter, being sure that some are close to the edges of the pan. Next, spoon out the reserved brownie batter close to some of the peanut butter filling. Using the tip of a sharp knife, swirl the two batters together to form a marble-like effect.

Bake 25–30 minutes or until a cake tester inserted into center of brownie comes out with moist crumbs attached. Remove from oven and immediately sprinkle the peanut butter chips evenly over top.

Allow to cool to room temperature, or overnight, before cutting and serving.

MAKES TWENTY-FOUR 3-INCH BROWNIES

Blondies with White and Dark Chocolate Chunks

A moist and chewy butterscotch bar with two kinds of chocolate and lots of walnuts.

1½ cups cake flour (not self-rising)
1 teaspoon baking powder
¼ teaspoon salt
¾ cup (1½ sticks) unsalted butter, softened
1 cup firmly packed light brown sugar
½ cup sugar

2 large eggs, at room temperature
2 teaspoons vanilla extract
1 cup coarsely chopped walnuts
¾ cup coarsely chopped white chocolate
½ cup coarsely chopped semisweet chocolate

Preheat oven to 350 degrees.

Grease and lightly flour a 13 x 9-inch baking pan.

In a small bowl, combine the flour, baking powder, and salt. Set aside.

In a large bowl, cream the butter with the sugars until smooth, about 2 minutes. Add the eggs and vanilla, and beat well. Add the dry ingredients and mix thoroughly. Stir in the walnuts and chocolate chunks. Spread the batter evenly in the prepared pan. Bake for 35–40 minutes, or until a cake tester inserted in the center of the pan comes out with moist crumbs attached. Do not overbake.

Allow to cool to room temperature or overnight before cutting and serving.

MAKES TWENTY-FOUR 2-INCH BLONDIES

Walnut Brown Sugar Squares

This is one of the quickest and easiest recipes in this book. You don't even need to wait for the butter to soften because there's no butter (or any shortening) in it!

½ cup plus 2 tablespoons all-purpose flour
¼ teaspoon baking soda
¼ teaspoon salt

1 cup firmly packed light brown sugar
1 large egg, at room temperature
1 teaspoon vanilla extract
1 cup chopped walnuts

Preheat oven to 350 degrees.

Lightly grease an 8 x 8-inch baking pan.

In a small bowl, combine the flour, baking soda, and salt. Set aside.

In a medium-size bowl, on the medium speed of an electric mixer, beat together the sugar, egg, and vanilla until creamy and smooth, about 2 minutes. Add the dry ingredients and mix thoroughly. Stir in the walnuts, reserving 2 tablespoons. Transfer the batter to the prepared pan and, using your hands, spread the batter evenly. Sprinkle with the remaining 2 tablespoons of walnuts. Bake for 25 minutes. The center will not be set but do not overbake.

Cool to room temperature, cover tightly with plastic wrap, and allow to set overnight before cutting and serving.

MAKES SIXTEEN 2-INCH SQUARES

Chocolate Brownies with Cream Cheese Icing

This cakey brownie will delight chocolate lovers from coast to coast. If you ice half the pan with cream cheese icing and the other half with our variation fudge frosting, you might not know which one to choose. Better yet, ice one brownie with both icings and you can have your cake and eat it, too!

BROWNIE

3 cups cake flour (not self-rising flour)
1 ½ teaspoons baking powder
1 ½ teaspoons salt
1 ½ cups (3 sticks) unsalted butter, softened
3 cups sugar
6 large eggs, at room temperature
1 tablespoon vanilla extract
9 ounces unsweetened chocolate, melted (see Note)

ICING

1 pound (2 eight-ounce packages) cream cheese, softened
6 tablespoons (¾ stick) unsalted butter, softened
1 ½ teaspoons vanilla extract
6 cups confectioners' sugar

GARNISH (OPTIONAL)

¾ cup coarsely chopped walnuts

NOTE: To melt chocolate, place in a double boiler over simmering water on low heat for approximately 5–10 minutes. Stir occasionally until completely smooth and no pieces of chocolate remain. Remove from heat and let cool for 5–10 minutes.

Preheat oven to 350 degrees.

Grease a 12 x 18-inch jelly roll pan.

To make the brownie: In a large bowl, sift together the flour, the baking powder, and the salt. Set aside.

In a large bowl, cream the butter and the sugar until fluffy, about 3 minutes. Lightly beat the eggs, then add to the creamed mixture and mix well. Add the vanilla. Add the chocolate and mix until well incorporated. Add the dry ingredients. Pour the batter into prepared pan. Bake 25–30 minutes or until a cake tester inserted into center of pan comes out with moist crumbs attached.

To make the icing: In a medium-size bowl, on the medium speed of an electric mixer, beat together the cream cheese and the butter until smooth, about 3 minutes. Add the vanilla extract. Gradually add the sugar and beat until well incorporated.

Let brownies cool completely, then ice with cream cheese icing.

As an optional icing, try this fudge frosting: In a small saucepan, combine ¾ cup heavy cream and 12 ounces semisweet chocolate and place over very low heat. Stir constantly until smooth. Remove from heat and stir in ¾ cup confectioners' sugar until dissolved. Allow to stand until firm.

MAKES TWENTY-FOUR 3-INCH BROWNIES

Hello Dolly Bars

After years of hearing customers and friends from the South tell her about a bar cookie that was just like the Magic Cookie Bar (see recipe on page 68) she serves at the bakery, Allysa finally received an actual recipe for Hello Dolly Bars from Maria Howard of Peculiar, Missouri. It turns out that the ingredients are a little different, and they're even easier to make—you just dump all the ingredients in a bowl and mix.

2 cups graham cracker crumbs

2 cups coarsely chopped pecans

2 cups sweetened shredded coconut

1 cup semisweet chocolate chips

1 cup butterscotch chips

¾ cup (1 ½ sticks) unsalted butter, melted

One and a half 14-ounce cans sweetened condensed milk

Preheat oven to 325 degrees.

Lightly grease a 13 x 9-inch baking pan.

Mix together all the ingredients except the sweetened condensed milk in a large bowl. Transfer the mixture to the prepared pan and pat down evenly with your hands. Pour the sweetened condensed milk over the top to cover, using a spatula to spread if necessary. Bake for 30–35 minutes, or until lightly golden. Cool to room temperature, cover tightly with plastic wrap, and allow to set overnight before cutting and serving.

MAKES TWENTY-FOUR 2-INCH BARS

Chocolate Brownies with Caramel, Peanut Butter, and Pecans

This is a variation on a brownie that we served at the bakery for years. In this version, though, the caramel and pecans, plus the surprisingly tasty addition of peanut butter chips, are layered between the graham cracker crust and the brownie.

CRUST
2¼ cups graham cracker crumbs
¾ cup (1½ sticks) unsalted butter, melted

CARAMEL FILLING
1 pound vanilla caramels
¼ cup heavy cream
¾ cup coarsely chopped toasted pecans (see Note)
½ cup peanut butter chips

BROWNIE
½ cup all-purpose flour
¾ teaspoon baking powder
½ teaspoon salt
½ cup (1 stick) unsalted butter
6 ounces unsweetened chocolate
1½ cups sugar
3 large eggs, at room temperature
1 teaspoon vanilla extract

NOTE: To toast the pecans, place on a baking sheet in a 350-degree oven for 15 minutes, or until lightly browned and fragrant.

Preheat oven to 350 degrees.

To make the crust: In a medium-size bowl, combine the graham cracker crumbs and melted butter. Press firmly into an ungreased 13 x 9-inch baking pan. Set aside.

To make the caramel filling: In a medium-size saucepan over low heat, melt the caramels with the cream, stirring occasionally, until smooth. Remove from the heat and pour over the graham cracker crust. Use a spatula to spread it evenly. Sprinkle the pecans and peanut butter chips over the caramel. Set aside.

To make the brownie: In a small bowl, combine the flour, baking powder, and salt. Set aside. In a medium-size saucepan over low heat, melt the butter and chocolate, stirring occasionally until smooth. Remove from the heat, transfer to a large bowl, and allow the mixture to cool for 5 minutes. Add the sugar, eggs, and vanilla, and beat well.

(continued)

Add the dry ingredients and mix thoroughly. Pour the batter over the pecans and peanut butter chips to completely cover the caramel layer. Bake for 35–45 minutes, or until a cake tester inserted in the center of the pan comes out with moist crumbs attached. Do not overbake.

Cool to room temperature, cover tightly with plastic wrap, and allow to set overnight before cutting and serving.

MAKES TWENTY-FOUR 2-INCH BROWNIES

CUPCAKES
AND
LAYER CAKES

Magnolia's Vanilla Cupcakes

Everyone was always asking us which was the most popular cupcake at the bakery. Most people were surprised that it was what we called the vanilla vanilla—the vanilla cupcake with the vanilla icing (and the most popular color for the icing was pink).

CUPCAKES
1 ½ cups self-rising flour
1 ¼ cups all-purpose flour
1 cup (2 sticks) unsalted butter,
     softened
2 cups sugar
4 large eggs, at room temperature

1 cup milk
1 teaspoon vanilla extract

ICING
Vanilla Buttercream (page 127) or
     Chocolate Buttercream (page 137)

NOTE: For layer cake instructions, see page 97.

Preheat oven to 350 degrees.

Line two 12-cup muffin tins with cupcake papers.

In a small bowl, combine the flours. Set aside.

In a large bowl, on the medium speed of an electric mixer, cream the butter until smooth. Add the sugar gradually and beat until fluffy, about 3 minutes. Add the eggs, one at a time, beating well after each addition. Add the dry ingredients in three parts, alternating with the milk and vanilla. With each addition, beat until the ingredients are incorporated but do not overbeat. Using a rubber spatula, scrape down the batter in the bowl to make sure the ingredients are well blended. Carefully spoon the batter into the cupcake liners, filling them about three-quarters full. Bake for 20–25 minutes, or until a cake tester inserted into the center of the cupcake comes out clean.

Cool the cupcakes in the tins for 15 minutes. Remove from the tins and cool completely on a wire rack before icing. At the bakery we iced the cupcakes with either Vanilla Buttercream or Chocolate Buttercream.

MAKES ABOUT 2 DOZEN CUPCAKES
(DEPENDING ON THE SIZE OF YOUR CUPCAKE PAPERS AND MUFFIN TINS)

Devil's Food Cake

At Allysa's house this cake was always iced with sweetened vanilla whipped cream. At the bakery we used a Mocha Buttercream. Whichever icing you choose, this devilishly rich chocolate cake is sure to be a hit.

3 cups all-purpose flour
1 ½ teaspoons baking powder
1 ½ teaspoons baking soda
¾ teaspoon salt
3 large eggs, separated, at
    room temperature
    (see first Note)

¾ cup (1 ½ sticks) unsalted butter,
    softened
2 cups firmly packed light brown sugar
8 ounces unsweetened chocolate,
    melted (see second Note)
2 cups milk
1 ½ teaspoons vanilla extract

NOTES: It is best to separate the eggs when cold and then allow them to come to room temperature before proceeding with the recipe.

To melt chocolate, place in a double boiler over simmering water on low heat for approximately 5–10 minutes. Stir occasionally until completely smooth and no pieces of chocolate remain. Remove from heat and let cool for 5–10 minutes.

Preheat oven to 350 degrees.

Grease and lightly flour two 9 x 2-inch round cake pans, then line the bottoms with waxed paper.

In a large bowl, sift together the flour, the baking powder, the baking soda, and the salt. Set aside.

Lightly beat the egg yolks until thick and lemon colored, about 2 minutes.

In a large bowl, cream the butter and the sugar until smooth, about 3 minutes. Add the egg yolks, beating until well combined. Add the chocolate, mixing until well incorporated. Add the dry ingredients in thirds, alternating with the milk and the vanilla, beating after each addition until smooth. In a separate bowl, beat the egg whites on the high speed of an electric mixer until soft peaks form. Gently fold into the batter. Divide the batter between the prepared pans and bake for 40–45 minutes or until a cake tester inserted into center of cake comes out clean. Let cakes cool in pans for 10 minutes. Remove from pans and cool completely on wire racks. When cake has cooled, ice between the layers, then ice top and sides of cake.

MAKES 1 TWO-LAYER 9-INCH CAKE

Black Bottom Cupcakes

During Allysa's quest in the kitchen for the perfect version of one of her favorite childhood treats, she was surprised to discover that many of her friends and neighbors (that is, testers) had never tried a black bottom cupcake before. If you're part of this group, you need to bake a batch—they're absolutely wonderful.

CREAM CHEESE FILLING
¾ pound (one and a half 8-ounce packages) cream cheese (not softened)
½ cup sugar
1 large egg, at room temperature
⅓ cup miniature semisweet chocolate chips

CUPCAKES
1¾ cups all-purpose flour
¾ cup unsweetened Dutch process cocoa
1 teaspoon baking soda
¼ teaspoon salt
½ cup vegetable oil (preferably canola)
1 cup sugar
1 cup buttermilk
2 teaspoons vanilla extract

Preheat oven to 350 degrees.

Line two 12-cup muffin tins with 18 cupcake papers.

To make the cream cheese filling: In a medium-size bowl, beat the cream cheese and sugar until smooth. Add the egg and beat well. Stir in the chocolate chips. Set aside.

To make the cupcakes: In a small bowl, combine the flour, cocoa, baking soda, and salt. Set aside. In a large bowl, on the medium speed of an electric mixer, beat together the oil and sugar. Add the dry ingredients in two parts, alternating with the buttermilk and vanilla, and making sure all ingredients are well blended.

Carefully spoon the cupcake batter into the cupcake liners, filling them about two-thirds full. Drop a small scoop (about 1½ tablespoons) of the cream cheese filling on top of each cupcake. Bake for 30–35 minutes, or until a cake tester inserted in the center of the cupcake comes out clean.

Cool the cupcakes in the tins for 30 minutes. Remove from the tins and cool completely on a wire rack.

MAKES 1½ DOZEN CUPCAKES

Coconut Layer Cake

Allysa has had this recipe in her cookbook for years. It's originally from a woman named Kathy who lives in the Midwest. It's a wonderful cake and became one of the all-time favorites among customers at the Magnolia Bakery. Kathy, we don't know you, but thanks a lot! This cake is best served the day it is filled and frosted.

CAKE
1 cup (2 sticks) unsalted butter, softened
2 cups sugar
4 large eggs, at room temperature
1 ½ cups self-rising flour
1 ¼ cups all-purpose flour
1 cup milk
1 teaspoon vanilla extract

FILLING
¾ cup milk
½ cup sugar
2 tablespoons all-purpose flour

1 seven-ounce package sweetened, shredded coconut
1 teaspoon vanilla extract

FROSTING
3 egg whites
1 ½ teaspoons vanilla extract
½ cup cold water
1 ½ cups sugar
¼ plus ⅛ teaspoon cream of tartar

GARNISH
Sweetened, shredded coconut

Preheat oven to 350 degrees.

Grease and lightly flour three 9 x 2-inch round cake pans, then line the bottoms with waxed paper.

To make the cake: In a large bowl, on the medium speed of an electric mixer, cream the butter until smooth. Add the sugar gradually and beat until fluffy, about 3 minutes. Add the eggs one at a time, beating well after each addition. Combine the flours and add in four parts, alternating with the milk and the vanilla extract, beating well after each addition. Divide the batter among the cake pans. Bake for 20–25 minutes or until a cake tester inserted into center of cake comes out clean. Let cakes cool in pans for 10 minutes. Remove from pans and cool completely on wire rack.

(continued)

To make the filling: In a medium-size saucepan, whisk the milk with the sugar and the flour until thoroughly combined. Cook and stir constantly over medium-high heat (about 5 minutes) until thickened and bubbly. Remove from heat and add the coconut. Stir in the vanilla. Cover and cool to room temperature.

When cake has cooled, spread half the filling between the first two layers of cake, then the other half between the second and third layers. The cake should be assembled so it can be iced as soon as the frosting is completed.

To make the frosting: In an electric mixer bowl, combine the egg whites and the vanilla and set aside. In a medium-size saucepan over high heat, combine the water with the sugar and the cream of tartar. As mixture begins to bubble at edges, stir once to make sure the sugar is dissolved completely, then let come to a rolling boil (about 2–3 minutes) and remove immediately from heat.

Now, in a medium-size bowl, on the medium-high speed of an electric mixer, beat the egg whites and the vanilla extract with the whisk attachment until foamy, about 1 minute.

Without turning off mixer, pour the sugar syrup into the beaten egg whites in a thin, steady stream. Continue beating constantly, on medium-high speed, for about 5 minutes or until stiff peaks form but frosting is still creamy. Frost top and sides of cake immediately.

Generously sprinkle top with shredded coconut.

MAKES 1 THREE-LAYER 9-INCH CAKE

Traditional Vanilla Birthday Cake

At Magnolia we decided to make our cake not quite a traditional yellow cake or a traditional sponge cake, given the use of whole eggs in our recipe. We're sure you'll agree this recipe is moist, delicious, and makes a beautiful layer cake or cupcakes for birthdays or any celebration. Frost with pink buttercream icing and lots of colored sprinkles, and feel as though you're at your seventh birthday party all over again!

1 cup (2 sticks) unsalted butter,
    softened
2 cups sugar
4 large eggs, at room temperature

1 ½ cups self-rising flour
1 ¼ cups all-purpose flour
1 cup milk
1 teaspoon vanilla extract

NOTE: For cupcake instructions, see the recipe on page 91.

Preheat oven to 350 degrees.

Grease and lightly flour three 9 x 2-inch round cake pans, then line the bottoms with waxed paper.

To make the cake: In a large bowl, on the medium speed of an electric mixer, cream the butter until smooth. Add the sugar gradually and beat until fluffy, about 3 minutes. Add the eggs one at a time, beating well after each addition. Combine the flours and add in four parts, alternating with the milk and the vanilla, beating well after each addition. Divide batter among the cake pans. Bake for 20–25 minutes or until a cake tester inserted into center of cake comes out clean. Let cakes cool in pans for ten minutes. Remove from pans and cool completely on wire rack.

When cake has cooled, ice between the layers, then ice top and sides of cake.

MAKES 1 THREE-LAYER 9-INCH CAKE OR 24 CUPCAKES

Devil's Food Cupcakes with Caramel Frosting

This recipe is very different from the devil's food cake recipe in later pages—more chocolaty and extremely light in texture. These cupcakes are great with the caramel frosting, but don't hesitate to try them with other icings as well.

CUPCAKES
2 cups cake flour (not self-rising)
1 cup unsweetened Dutch process cocoa
1½ teaspoons baking soda
½ teaspoon salt
¾ cup (1½ sticks) unsalted butter, softened

1½ cups firmly packed light brown sugar
½ cup sugar
3 large eggs, at room temperature
1½ cups buttermilk
2 teaspoons vanilla extract

FROSTING
1 recipe Caramel Frosting (page 134)

Preheat oven to 350 degrees.

Line three 12-cup muffin tins with cupcake papers. Set aside.

In a small bowl, sift together the flour, cocoa, baking soda, and salt. Set aside.

In a large bowl, on the medium speed of an electric mixer, cream the butter until smooth. Add the sugars and beat until fluffy, about 3 minutes. Add the eggs, one at a time, beating well after each addition. Add the dry ingredients in three parts, alternating with the buttermilk and vanilla. With each addition, beat until the ingredients are incorporated, but do not overbeat. Using a rubber spatula, scrape down the batter in the bowl, making sure the ingredients are well blended. Carefully spoon the batter into the cupcake liners, filling them about three-quarters full. Bake for 25–30 minutes, or until a cake tester inserted in the center of the cupcake comes out clean.

Cool the cupcakes in the tins for 15 minutes. Remove from the tins and cool completely on a wire rack before icing with Caramel Frosting.

MAKES ABOUT 2¼ DOZEN CUPCAKES
(DEPENDING ON THE SIZE OF YOUR CUPCAKE PAPERS AND MUFFIN TINS)

Old-Fashioned White Cake

Here's a terrific cake with a wonderful texture. It uses only egg whites, so it's ideal for the cholesterol-conscious. Try it with as many icings as you can think of—you can't go wrong!

½ cup (1 stick) unsalted butter, softened
1 ½ cups sugar
2 cups self-rising flour

1 cup milk
2 teaspoons vanilla extract
4 large egg whites

Preheat oven to 350 degrees.

Grease and lightly flour two 9 x 2-inch round cake pans, then line the bottoms with waxed paper.

To make the cake: In a large bowl, on the medium speed of an electric mixer, cream the butter until smooth. Add the sugar gradually and beat until fluffy, about 3 minutes. Add the flour in three parts, alternating with the milk and the vanilla, beating well after each addition. In a separate bowl, on the high speed of an electric mixer, beat the egg whites until soft peaks form. Gently fold into batter, making sure no streaks of whites are showing. Divide batter between the cake pans. Bake for 22–25 minutes or until a cake tester inserted into center of cake comes out clean. Let cakes cool in pans for 10 minutes. Remove from pans and cool completely on wire rack.

When cake has cooled, ice between the layers, then ice top and sides of cake.

MAKES 1 TWO-LAYER 9-INCH CAKE

Apple Walnut Cake with Caramel Cream Cheese Icing

We made this exceptionally pretty cake for special orders only, but so many customers requested it that it became part of our standard cake repertoire. It's perfect for an autumn dinner party or as a delicious alternative to a Thanksgiving pie.

CAKE

2 cups all-purpose flour
1 cup whole-wheat flour
1 teaspoon cinnamon
1 teaspoon baking soda
¾ teaspoon salt
1½ cups vegetable oil
2 cups sugar
3 large eggs, at room temperature
3 cups (3 large) Golden Delicious apples, cut into 1-inch pieces
1 cup coarsely chopped walnuts
3 tablespoons apple-flavored brandy

ICING

1 pound (2 eight-ounce packages) cream cheese, softened slightly, cut into pieces
½ cup (1 stick) unsalted butter, softened slightly, cut into pieces
1 cup cold caramel, plus extra (about ¼ cup) for decorating (recipe on page 140)

GARNISH

Coarsely chopped or whole walnuts

Preheat oven to 325 degrees.

Grease and lightly flour two 9 x 2-inch round cake pans, then line the bottoms with waxed paper.

To make the cake: In a large bowl, sift together the flours, the cinnamon, the baking soda, and the salt. Set aside.

In a large bowl, on the medium speed of an electric mixer, beat the oil with the sugar until smooth, about 3 minutes. Add the eggs one at a time and beat until light, about 1 or 2 minutes. Add the dry ingredients in thirds, beating after each addition until smooth. The batter will be extremely thick and doughlike. With a spoon, stir in the apples, the walnuts, and the brandy until just blended. Divide the batter between the prepared pans and bake for 45–55 minutes or until a cake tester inserted into center of cake comes out clean. Let cakes cool in pans for 10 minutes. Remove from pans and cool completely on wire rack.

To make the icing: In a medium-size bowl, on the medium speed of an electric mixer, beat the cream cheese and the butter until smooth, about 3 minutes. Gradually add the caramel and beat until well incorporated.

When cake has cooled, ice between the layers, then ice top and sides of cake. Drizzle remaining caramel over top of cake, and using a small knife, swirl caramel into icing, forming a decorative pattern. Garnish with walnuts as desired.

MAKES 1 TWO-LAYER 9-INCH CAKE

Carrot Cake

We didn't make carrot cake at the bakery (I can just hear the Hummingbird Cake fans screaming), but this is a cake that Allysa makes often at home. She just loves it.

CAKE
2 cups all-purpose flour
1 teaspoon baking powder
1 teaspoon cinnamon
½ teaspoon salt
1 cup vegetable oil (preferably canola)
1¾ cups sugar
3 large eggs, at room temperature
1½ teaspoons vanilla extract
2 cups lightly packed shredded carrots
One 8-ounce can crushed pineapple in
     its own juice, with juice

1 cup coarsely chopped toasted
     pecans (see Note)
¾ cup sweetened shredded coconut

ICING
1 recipe Cream Cheese Icing
     (page 128)

GARNISH
Coarsely chopped toasted pecans
     (see Note)

NOTE: To toast the pecans, place on a baking sheet in a 350-degree oven for 15 minutes, or until lightly browned and fragrant.

Preheat oven to 325 degrees.

Grease and lightly flour two 9 x 2-inch round cake pans, then line the bottoms with waxed paper.

In a small bowl, sift together the flour, baking powder, cinnamon, and salt. Set aside.

In a large bowl, on the medium speed of an electric mixer, beat together the oil and sugar. Add the eggs, one at a time, and beat until light and thick, about 2 minutes. Add the vanilla and beat well. Gradually add the dry ingredients, beating until well incorporated. Stir in the carrots, pineapple and juice, pecans, and coconut. Divide the batter between the prepared pans and bake for 40–50 minutes, or until a cake tester inserted in the center of the cake comes out clean. Let the layers cool in the pans for 1 hour. Remove from the pans and cool completely on a wire rack.

When the cake has cooled, ice between the layers, then ice the top and sides of the cake with Cream Cheese Icing. Garnish with the toasted pecans as desired.

MAKES ONE 2-LAYER 9-INCH CAKE

Devil's Food Cake with Seven-Minute Icing and Coconut

This is the same recipe Allysa's family has made for every birthday since the beginning of time, and the same cake we served at the bakery—but a different icing and the coconut garnish give it a whole new taste.

CAKE
3 cups all-purpose flour
1 ½ teaspoons baking powder
1 ½ teaspoons baking soda
¾ teaspoon salt
¾ cup (1 ½ sticks) unsalted butter, softened
2 cups firmly packed light brown sugar
3 large eggs, separated, at room temperature (see first Note)

9 ounces unsweetened chocolate, melted (see second Note)
2 cups milk
1 ½ teaspoons vanilla extract

ICING
One recipe Seven-Minute Icing (page 132)

GARNISH
Sweetened shredded coconut

NOTES: It is best to separate the eggs when cold and then allow them to come to room temperature before proceeding with the recipe.

To melt the chocolate, place in a double boiler over simmering water on low heat for approximately 5–10 minutes. Stir occasionally until completely smooth and no pieces of chocolate remain. Remove from the heat and let cool to lukewarm, 5–10 minutes.

Preheat oven to 350 degrees.

Grease and lightly flour three 9 x 2-inch round cake pans, then line the bottoms with waxed paper.

In a small bowl, sift together the flour, baking powder, baking soda, and salt. Set aside.

In a large bowl, on the medium speed of an electric mixer, cream the butter until smooth. Add the sugar and beat until fluffy, about 3 minutes.

In a separate small bowl, beat the egg yolks until thick and lemon-colored, about 2 minutes. Add the beaten yolks to the butter mixture and beat well. Add the chocolate, mixing until well incorporated. Add the dry ingredients in three parts, alternating with the milk and vanilla. With each addition, beat until the ingredients are incorporated, but do not overbeat. Using a rubber spatula, scrape down the batter in the bowl, making sure the ingredients are well blended and the batter is smooth.

In a separate small bowl, beat the egg whites on the high speed of an electric mixer until soft peaks form. Gently fold into the batter. Divide the batter among the prepared pans and bake for 30–35 minutes, or until a cake tester inserted in the center of the cake comes out clean.

Let the layers cool in the pans for 1 hour. Remove from the pans and cool completely on a wire rack.

When the cake has cooled, ice between the layers, then ice the top and sides of the cake with Seven-Minute Icing. Sprinkle the top of the cake generously with the coconut.

MAKES ONE 3-LAYER 9-INCH CAKE

Lemon Layer Cake

This moist and fluffy cake is equally delicious with Lemon Buttercream (page 133) or Lemon Curd filling (page 139).

1 cup (2 sticks) unsalted butter, softened
2 cups sugar
4 large eggs, at room temperature
1 ½ cups self-rising flour

1 ¼ cups all-purpose flour
¾ cup milk
¼ cup fresh lemon juice
2 teaspoons grated lemon zest

Preheat oven to 350 degrees.

Grease and lightly flour three 9 x 2-inch round cake pans, then line the bottoms with waxed paper.

To make the cake: In a large bowl, on the medium speed of an electric mixer, cream the butter until smooth. Add the sugar gradually and beat until fluffy, about 3 minutes. Add the eggs one at a time. Combine the flours and add in four parts, alternating with the milk and the lemon juice and zest, beating well after each addition. Divide the batter among the cake pans. Bake for 20–25 minutes or until a cake tester inserted into center of cake comes out clean. Let cakes cool in pans for 10 minutes. Remove from pans and cool completely on wire rack.

When cake has cooled, spread the icing or the curd evenly between layers and over top of cake.

MAKES 1 THREE-LAYER 9-INCH CAKE

Apple Cake with Butterscotch Cream Cheese Frosting

A fluffy, golden cake with chunks of apples and a sweet, creamy frosting. If you're not a butterscotch fan, this cake is also good iced with vanilla buttercream.

CAKE

3 cups all-purpose flour
2 teaspoons baking powder
½ teaspoon salt
1 cup (2 sticks) unsalted butter, softened
2 cups sugar
5 large eggs, at room temperature
1 cup milk
1 ½ teaspoons vanilla extract
3 ½ cups coarsely chopped, peeled, crisp tart apples (such as Winesap or Macoun)

FROSTING

1 recipe Butterscotch Cream Cheese Frosting (page 136)

Preheat oven to 325 degrees.

Grease and lightly flour two 9-inch round cake pans, then line the bottoms with waxed paper.

In a small bowl, sift together the flour, baking powder, and salt. Set aside. In a large bowl, on the medium speed of an electric mixer, cream the butter until smooth. Add the sugar gradually and beat until fluffy, about 3 minutes. Add the eggs, one at a time, beating well after each addition. Add the dry ingredients in three parts, alternating with the milk and vanilla. With each addition, beat until the ingredients are incorporated, but do not overbeat. Using a rubber spatula, scrape down the batter in the bowl, making sure the ingredients are well blended. Stir in the apples.

Divide the batter between the prepared pans. Bake for 40–50 minutes, or until a cake tester inserted in the center of the cake comes out clean.

Let the layers cool in the pans for 1 hour. Remove from the pans and cool completely on a wire rack.

When the cake has cooled, ice between the layers, then ice top and sides of cake with Butterscotch Cream Cheese Frosting.

MAKES ONE 2-LAYER 9-INCH CAKE

Magnolia's Chocolate Cupcakes

Made from the same batter as our popular Chocolate Buttermilk Cake, this not too rich and not too chocolaty cupcake goes equally well with the Vanilla or Chocolate Buttercream Icing.

CUPCAKES
2 cups all-purpose flour
1 teaspoon baking soda
1 cup (2 sticks) unsalted butter, softened
1 cup sugar
1 cup firmly packed light brown sugar
4 large eggs, at room temperature

6 ounces unsweetened chocolate, melted (see Note)
1 cup buttermilk
1 teaspoon vanilla extract

ICINGS
Vanilla Buttercream (page 127) or Chocolate Buttercream (page 137)

NOTE: To melt the chocolate, place in a double boiler over simmering water on low heat for approximately 5–10 minutes. Stir occasionally until completely smooth and no pieces of chocolate remain. Remove from the heat and let cool to lukewarm 5–10 minutes.

For layer cake instructions see the recipe on page 112.

Preheat oven to 350 degrees.

Line two 12-cup muffin tins with cupcake papers. Set aside.

In a small bowl, sift together the flour and baking soda. Set aside.

In a large bowl, on the medium speed of an electric mixer, cream the butter until smooth. Add the sugars and beat until fluffy, about 3 minutes. Add the eggs, one at a time, beating well after each addition. Add the chocolate, mixing until well incorporated. Add the dry ingredients in three parts, alternating with the buttermilk and vanilla. With each addition, beat until the ingredients are incorporated, but do not overbeat. Using a rubber spatula, scrape down the batter in the bowl to make sure the ingredients are well blended and the batter is smooth. Carefully spoon the batter into the cupcake liners, filling them about three-quarters full. Bake for 20–25 minutes, or until a cake tester inserted in the center of the cupcake comes out clean.

Cool the cupcakes in the tins for 15 minutes. Remove from the tins and cool completely on a wire rack before icing. At the bakery we iced the cupcakes with either Vanilla Buttercream or Chocolate Buttercream.

MAKES ABOUT 2 DOZEN CUPCAKES
(DEPENDING ON THE SIZE OF YOUR CUPCAKE PAPERS AND MUFFIN TINS)

Strawberry Shortcake

Here is an old-fashioned favorite that doesn't seem to go out of style. Allysa recommends serving this cake relatively soon after assembling it, since the whipped cream tends to melt a little in the warm weather. She never refrigerates cakes because they dry out quickly when chilled.

CAKE
1 ½ cups self-rising flour
1 ¼ cups all-purpose flour
1 cup (2 sticks) unsalted butter, softened
2 cups sugar
4 large eggs, at room temperature
1 cup milk
1 teaspoon vanilla extract

CREAM FILLING
2 cups heavy cream
¼ cup confectioners' sugar
2 teaspoons vanilla extract

BERRY FILLING
2 pints (4 cups) ripe strawberries, sliced in half
2 tablespoons sugar

Preheat oven to 350 degrees.

Grease and lightly flour three 9 x 2-inch round cake pans, then line the bottoms with waxed paper.

To make the cake: In a small bowl, combine the flours and set aside. In a large bowl, on the medium speed of an electric mixer, cream the butter until smooth. Add the sugar gradually and beat until fluffy, about 3 minutes. Add the eggs, one at a time, beating well after each addition. Add the dry ingredients in three parts, alternating with the milk and vanilla. With each addition, beat until the ingredients are incorporated, but do not overbeat. Using a rubber spatula, scrape down the batter in the bowl, making sure the ingredients are well blended.

Divide the batter among the prepared pans and bake for 25–30 minutes, or until a cake tester inserted in the center of the cake comes out clean. Let the layers cool in the pans for 1 hour. Remove from the pans and cool completely on a wire rack.

To make the cream filling: In a large bowl, whip the heavy cream with the sugar and vanilla until stiff peaks form.

To make the berry filling: Gently toss the berries with the sugar to evenly coat the fruit.

To assemble the cake: When the cake layers have cooled completely, spread one-third of the whipped cream filling over the bottom cake layer, followed by one-third of the berry filling. Repeat with the remaining layers.

MAKES ONE 3-LAYER 9-INCH CAKE

Chocolate Buttermilk Layer Cake

We think this is the ideal chocolate layer cake. Moist and tender, this cake has a beautiful texture and a taste that's out of this world!

2 cups all-purpose flour

1 teaspoon baking soda

1 cup (2 sticks) unsalted butter, softened

1 cup sugar

1 cup firmly packed light brown sugar

4 large eggs, at room temperature

6 ounces unsweetened chocolate, melted (see Note)

1 cup buttermilk

1 teaspoon vanilla extract

NOTES: To melt chocolate, place in a double boiler over simmering water on low heat for approximately 5–10 minutes. Stir occasionally until completely smooth and no pieces of chocolate remain. Remove from heat and let cool for 5–10 minutes.

For cupcake instructions, see recipe on page 108.

Preheat oven to 350 degrees.

Grease and lightly flour two 9 x 2-inch round cake pans, then line the bottoms with waxed paper.

In a medium-size bowl, sift together the flour and the baking soda. Set aside.

In a large bowl, cream the butter and the sugars until smooth, about 3 minutes. Add the eggs one at a time, beating well after each addition. Add the chocolate, mixing until well incorporated. Add the dry ingredients in thirds, alternating with the buttermilk and the vanilla, beating after each addition until smooth. Divide the batter between the prepared pans and bake for 25–35 minutes or until a cake tester inserted into center of cake comes out clean. Let cakes cool in pans for 10 minutes. Remove from pans and cool completely on wire racks.

When cake has cooled, ice between the layers, then ice top and sides of cake. At the bakery we iced this cake with either traditional Vanilla or Chocolate Buttercream (pages 127 or 137).

MAKES 1 TWO-LAYER 9-INCH CAKE

Red Velvet Cake with Creamy Vanilla Frosting

This was one of our most popular cakes at the bakery. Half of the customers loved it because they hadn't eaten it since their grandmother made it when they were kids, and the other half because they thought the red color was really neat. But everyone thinks it's delicious.

CAKE
3⅓ cups cake flour (not self-rising)
¾ cup (1½ sticks) unsalted butter, softened
2¼ cups sugar
3 large eggs, at room temperature
6 tablespoons red food coloring
3 tablespoons unsweetened cocoa
1½ teaspoons vanilla extract

1½ teaspoons salt
1½ cups buttermilk
1½ teaspoons cider vinegar
1½ teaspoons baking soda

FROSTING
1 recipe Creamy Vanilla Frosting (page 130)

Preheat oven to 350 degrees.

Grease and lightly flour three 9 x 2-inch round cake pans, then line the bottoms with waxed paper.

To make the cake: In a small bowl, sift the cake flour and set aside. In a large bowl, on the medium speed of an electric mixer, cream the butter and sugar until very light and fluffy, about 5 minutes. Add the eggs, one at a time, beating well after each addition.

In a small bowl, whisk together the red food coloring, cocoa, and vanilla. Add to the batter and beat well.

In a measuring cup, stir the salt into the buttermilk. Add to the batter in three parts, alternating with the flour. With each addition, beat until the ingredients are incorporated, but do not overbeat.

In a small bowl, stir together the cider vinegar and baking soda. Add to the batter and mix well. Using a rubber spatula, scrape down the batter in the bowl, making sure the ingredients are well blended and the batter is smooth.

(continued)

Divide the batter among the prepared pans. Bake for 30–40 minutes, or until a cake tester inserted in the center of the cake comes out clean. Let the layers cool in the pans for 1 hour. Remove from the pans and cool completely on a wire rack.

When the cake has cooled, spread the frosting between the layers, then ice the top and sides of the cake with Creamy Vanilla Frosting.

MAKES ONE 3-LAYER 9-INCH CAKE

Banana Cake with White Chocolate Cream Cheese Icing

This recipe came about because Allysa wanted to make a banana cake using butter instead of the traditional oil as the shortening. The result is a cake with a very different and quite lovely texture, and it's perfectly complemented by the white chocolate icing.

CAKE

3 cups cake flour (not self-rising)
1 teaspoon baking soda
¾ teaspoon salt
½ teaspoon baking powder
1 cup (2 sticks) unsalted butter, softened
2 cups sugar
3 large eggs, at room temperature
1½ cups mashed very ripe bananas

6 tablespoons buttermilk
1½ teaspoons vanilla extract

ICING

1 recipe White Chocolate Cream Cheese Icing (page 138)

GARNISH

¾ cup chopped walnuts or walnut halves

Preheat oven to 325 degrees.

Grease and lightly flour two 9 x 2-inch round cake pans, then line the bottoms with waxed paper.

To make the cake: In a small bowl, sift together the flour, baking soda, salt, and baking powder. Set aside.

In a large bowl, on the medium speed of an electric mixer, cream the butter until smooth. Add the sugar gradually and beat until fluffy, about 3 minutes. Add the eggs, one at a time, beating well after each addition. Add the bananas. Add half of the dry ingredients, mixing until well incorporated, then add the buttermilk and vanilla, and then the second half of the dry ingredients, mixing well. Divide the batter between the prepared pans. Bake for 40–50 minutes, or until a cake tester inserted in the center of the cake comes out clean.

(continued)

Let the layers cool in the pans for 1 hour. Remove from the pans and cool completely on a wire rack.

When the cake has cooled, ice between the layers with White Chocolate Cream Cheese Icing, then ice the top and sides of the cake. Garnish with the walnuts as desired.

MAKES ONE 2-LAYER 9-INCH CAKE

German Chocolate Cake

We confess we've improved on a classic recipe. Baker's German's Sweet Chocolate is the chocolate of choice for this cake.

CAKE

1 package (4 ounces) Baker's German's Sweet Chocolate, broken into squares
½ cup water
2 cups all-purpose flour
1 ½ teaspoons baking soda
¼ teaspoon salt
4 large eggs, separated, at room temperature (see Note)
1 cup (2 sticks) unsalted butter, softened
2 cups sugar

1 teaspoon vanilla extract
1 cup buttermilk

CARAMEL PECAN FILLING AND FROSTING

1 ½ cans (18 ounces) evaporated milk
6 egg yolks
2 cups sugar
1 cup (2 sticks) unsalted butter, cut into small pieces
2 teaspoons vanilla extract
4 cups sweetened, shredded coconut
2 cups coarsely chopped pecans

NOTE: It is best to separate the eggs when cold and then allow them to come to room temperature before proceeding with the recipe.

Preheat oven to 350 degrees.

Grease and lightly flour three 9 x 2-inch round cake pans, then line the bottoms with waxed paper.

To make the cake: In a small saucepan over low heat, combine the chocolate with the water, stirring to melt the chocolate, and blend well. Set aside to cool for 10 minutes.

Meanwhile, in a medium-size bowl, sift together the flour, the baking soda, and the salt. Set aside.

In a small bowl, lightly beat the egg yolks, about 1 minute.

In a large bowl, on the medium speed of an electric mixer, cream the butter and the sugar until light and fluffy, about 3 minutes. Add the egg yolks, beating until well com-

(continued)

bined. Add the chocolate mixture and the vanilla. Add the dry ingredients in thirds, alternating with the buttermilk, beating after each addition, until smooth. In a separate bowl, beat the egg whites on the high speed of an electric mixer until soft peaks form. Gently fold into batter. Divide batter among the prepared pans. Bake for 25–30 minutes or until a cake tester inserted into center of cake comes out clean. Be careful not to overbake, as this cake has a different, lighter texture than most.

Let cake cool in pans for 10 minutes. Remove from pans and cool completely on wire rack.

To make the frosting: In a large saucepan, beat together the evaporated milk and the egg yolks. Stir in the sugar, the butter, and the vanilla. Stir over medium heat about 15–18 minutes or until thickened and bubbly and golden in color. Remove from heat. Stir in the coconut and the pecans. Transfer to a large bowl and cool until room temperature and of good spreading consistency (about 2 hours; frosting will thicken as it cools).

When cake has cooled, spread frosting between layers and over top of cake.

MAKES 1 THREE-LAYER 9-INCH CAKE

Caramel Pecan Layer Cake

A light, moist vanilla cake iced with creamy caramel frosting and generous amounts of toasted pecans. It is a wonderful birthday cake alternative if you want to serve something different from the traditional yellow or chocolate cake.

CAKE
1 ½ cups self-rising flour
1 ¼ cups all-purpose flour
1 cup (2 sticks) unsalted butter,
    softened
2 cups sugar
4 large eggs, at room temperature
1 cup milk

1 teaspoon vanilla extract

ICING
1 recipe Caramel Frosting (page 134)

GARNISH
1 ½ cups coarsely chopped toasted
    pecans (see Note)

NOTE: To toast the pecans, place on a baking sheet in a 350-degree oven for 15 minutes, or until lightly browned and fragrant.

Preheat oven to 350 degrees.

Grease and lightly flour three 9 x 2-inch round cake pans, then line the bottoms with waxed paper.

To make the cake: In a small bowl, combine the flours and set aside. In a large bowl, on the medium speed of an electric mixer, cream the butter until smooth. Add the sugar gradually and beat until fluffy, about 3 minutes. Add the eggs, one at a time, beating well after each addition. Add the dry ingredients in three parts, alternating with the milk and vanilla. With each addition, beat until the ingredients are incorporated, but do not overbeat. Using a rubber spatula, scrape down the batter in the bowl, making sure the ingredients are well blended.

Divide the batter among the prepared pans and bake for 25–30 minutes, or until a cake tester inserted in the center of the cake comes out clean. Let the layers cool in the pans for 1 hour. Remove from the pans and cool completely on a wire rack.

(*continued*)

When the layers have cooled completely, ice the cake by filling between the layers first with Caramel Frosting and then sprinkling with one-third of the pecans on each layer. Then ice the top and sides, and sprinkle the top with the remaining pecans.

MAKES ONE 3-LAYER 9-INCH CAKE

Hummingbird Cake

This wonderful cake, filled with bananas, pineapples, and pecans, came our way by good fortune. One of our customers came into the bakery one afternoon with this recipe from his aunt, handwritten on an index card. He said she thought it would be a perfect cake for our bakery; she was right!

CAKE
3 cups all-purpose flour
1 teaspoon cinnamon
1 teaspoon baking soda
1 teaspoon salt
1¼ cups vegetable oil
2 cups sugar
3 large eggs, at room temperature
1½ teaspoons vanilla extract
2 cups mashed, very ripe bananas

1 eight-ounce can crushed pineapple
    in unsweetened juice, drained
    (about 1 cup)
½ cup chopped pecans

FROSTING
1 recipe Cream Cheese Icing
    (page 128)

GARNISH
Coarsely chopped or whole pecans

Preheat oven to 325 degrees.

Grease and lightly flour two 9 x 2-inch round cake pans, then line the bottoms with waxed paper.

To make the cake: In a large bowl, sift together the flour, the cinnamon, the baking soda, and the salt. Set aside.

In a large bowl, on the medium speed of an electric mixer, beat the oil with the sugar until smooth, about 3 minutes. Add the eggs one at a time and beat until light, about 1 or 2 minutes. Add the vanilla. Add the bananas and the pineapple. Add the dry ingredients in thirds, beating after each addition until smooth. Stir in the pecans. Divide the batter between the prepared pans and bake for 40–50 minutes or until a cake tester inserted into center of cake comes out clean. Let cakes cool in pans for 10 minutes. Remove from pans and cool completely on wire rack.

When cake has cooled, ice between the layers, then ice top and sides of cake with our Cream Cheese Icing. Garnish with pecans as desired.

MAKES 1 TWO-LAYER 9-INCH CAKE

Maple Walnut Layer Cake with Fluffy Maple Frosting

Here's a delicious twist on a vanilla cake Jennifer found in a vintage cookbook from 1954. The secret flavor is a hint of ginger. The frosting is a seven-minute icing made on the top of the stove. You must beat it continuously, but it's quick and easy, and the results are worth it!

CAKE
3¾ cups self-rising flour
½ teaspoon ginger
¾ cup (1½ sticks) unsalted butter, softened
½ cup sugar
3 large eggs, at room temperature
1½ cups pure maple syrup
¾ cup hot water

FROSTING
2 egg whites
½ cup maple syrup
¾ cup sugar
¼ teaspoon cream of tartar
¼ teaspoon salt
1 teaspoon vanilla extract
¼ teaspoon maple extract

GARNISH
1 cup chopped walnuts

Preheat oven to 350 degrees.

Grease and lightly flour two 9 x 2-inch round cake pans, then line the bottoms with waxed paper.

To make the cake: In a large bowl, sift together the flour and the ginger and set aside.

In a large bowl, cream the butter and the sugar until fluffy, about 3 minutes. Add the eggs one at a time, beating until well combined. Beat in the maple syrup gradually. Add the flour mixture in thirds, alternating with the water, beating after each addition until smooth. Divide the batter between the prepared pans and bake for 30–35 minutes or until a cake tester inserted into center of cake comes out clean.

Let cakes cool in pans for 10 minutes. Remove from pans and cool completely on wire rack.

To make the frosting: In the top of a double boiler, combine first five ingredients. Cook over boiling water, beating constantly on the medium-high speed of an electric mixer, until mixture stands in peaks (about 5–7 minutes). Remove the pot from heat. Add the vanilla and the maple extracts and continue beating 1 minute more until thick enough to spread.

When cake has cooled, ice between the layers. Sprinkle about ⅓ cup chopped walnuts over the frosting. Then ice top and sides of cake, sprinkling the top with the remaining chopped walnuts.

MAKES 1 TWO-LAYER 9-INCH CAKE

ICINGS, FILLINGS, FROSTINGS, AND SAUCES

Vanilla Buttercream

The vanilla buttercream we used at the bakery is technically not a buttercream but actually an old-fashioned confectioners' sugar and butter frosting. Be sure to beat the icing for the amount of time called for in the recipe to achieve the desired creamy texture.

1 cup (2 sticks) unsalted butter,
   softened
6–8 cups confectioners' sugar

½ cup milk
2 teaspoons vanilla extract

Place the butter in a large mixing bowl. Add 4 cups of the sugar and then the milk and vanilla. On the medium speed of an electric mixer, beat until smooth and creamy, about 3–5 minutes. Gradually add the remaining sugar, 1 cup at a time, beating well after each addition (about 2 minutes), until the icing is thick enough to be of good spreading consistency. You may not need to add all of the sugar. If desired, add a few drops of food coloring and mix thoroughly. (Use and store the icing at room temperature because icing will set if chilled.) Icing can be stored in an airtight container for up to 3 days.

MAKES ENOUGH FOR ONE 2-LAYER 9-INCH CAKE OR 2 DOZEN CUPCAKES

NOTE: If you are icing a 3-layer cake, use the following recipe proportions:

1 ½ cups (3 sticks) unsalted butter
8–10 cups confectioners' sugar

¾ cup milk
1 tablespoon vanilla extract

Cream Cheese Icing

We haven't found anyone who doesn't like cream cheese icing. It's the traditional icing for carrot cake, but is delicious with many other desserts as well.

1 pound (two 8-ounce packages) cream cheese, softened and cut into small pieces

6 tablespoons unsalted butter, softened and cut into small pieces

1½ teaspoons vanilla extract

5 cups sifted confectioners' sugar

In a large bowl, on the medium speed of an electric mixer, beat the cream cheese and butter until smooth, about 3 minutes. Add the vanilla and beat well. Gradually add the sugar, 1 cup at a time, beating continuously until smooth and creamy. Cover and refrigerate icing for 2 to 3 hours, but no longer, to thicken before using.

MAKES ENOUGH FOR ONE 2- OR 3-LAYER 9-INCH CAKE

Magnolia's Vanilla and Chocolate Cupcakes
with Vanilla Buttercream

Red Velvet Cake
with Creamy Vanilla Frosting

Pumpkin Cheesecake
with Gingersnap Pecan Crust

Raspberry Cream Cheese Breakfast Buns,
Nectarine Double-Crust Pie, Vanilla Cake with Vanilla Buttercream,
Chocolate Cake with Vanilla Buttercream

Vanilla Sandwich Creme Cookie Ice Cream,
White Chocolate Peanut Brittle Ice Cream,
Old-Fashioned Chocolate Chip Ice Cream

Apple Tart
with Hazelnut Brown Sugar Topping

IN THE JARS: Coconut Oatmeal Drop Cookies, Chocolate Chocolate Chip Drop Cookies,
Peanut Butter Chocolate Chip Pecan Cookies
ON THE CAKE STAND: Iced Ginger Cookies, White Chocolate Pecan Drop Cookies,
Blondies with Cream Cheese Swirl and Pecans
ON THE PLATE: Coconut Pecan Shortbread Squares, Chocolate Fudge Brownies with
Butterscotch Chips and Pecans, White Chocolate Pecan Drop Cookies

Devil's Food Cake
with Seven-Minute Icing and Coconut

Chocolate Glaze

A simple glaze (or ganache) that is great to pour over any desired dessert; we suggest it over our Chocolate Sour Cream Cake with Chocolate Chips (page 34), or our Chocolate Amaretto Bundt Cake (page 30).

4 ounces semisweet
  chocolate
4 tablespoons butter or
  cream

1–2 tablespoons liquor or liqueur
  of your choice (bourbon, rum,
  Grand Marnier, amaretto, brandy,
  and so on)

In a medium-size saucepan over low heat, melt the chocolate and the butter or cream, stirring occasionally until completely melted. Remove from heat and stir in desired liquor. Use immediately over completely cooled dessert. Allow to set for 15 minutes. Can be refrigerated and reheated gently if necessary.

THIS YIELDS ENOUGH GLAZE TO COVER ONE 10-INCH TUBE OR BUNDT CAKE

Creamy Vanilla Frosting

This silky smooth frosting is made by beating together softened butter and sugar with a thick, saucelike base. Be sure to follow the recipe directions exactly.

6 tablespoons all-purpose flour
2 cups milk
2 cups (4 sticks) unsalted butter,
    softened

2 cups sugar
2 teaspoons vanilla extract

In a medium-size saucepan, whisk the flour into the milk until smooth. Place over medium heat and, stirring constantly, cook until the mixture becomes very thick and begins to bubble, 10–15 minutes. Cover with waxed paper placed directly on the surface and cool to room temperature, about 30 minutes.

In a large bowl, on the medium high speed of an electric mixer, beat the butter for 3 minutes, until smooth and creamy. Gradually add the sugar, beating continuously for 3 minutes until fluffy. Add the vanilla and beat well.

Add the cooled milk mixture, and continue to beat on the medium high speed for 5 minutes, until very smooth and noticeably whiter in color. Cover and refrigerate for 15 minutes (no less and no longer—set a timer!). Use immediately.

MAKES ENOUGH FOR ONE 3-LAYER 9-INCH CAKE

White Chocolate Buttercream

This recipe is ideal for people who prefer white chocolate to chocolate, and the visual contrast of the white icing with a chocolate or devil's food cake is wonderful.

1 ½ cups (3 sticks) unsalted butter, softened
6 tablespoons milk
9 ounces white chocolate, melted and cooled to lukewarm (see Note)

1 teaspoon vanilla extract
3 cups sifted confectioners' sugar

NOTE: To melt the chocolate, place in a double boiler over simmering water on low heat for about 5–10 minutes. Stir occasionally until completely smooth and no pieces of chocolate remain. Remove from the heat and let cool for 5–15 minutes, or until lukewarm.

In a large bowl, on the medium speed of an electric mixer, beat the butter until creamy, about 3 minutes. Add the milk carefully and beat until smooth. Add the melted chocolate and beat well, about 2 minutes. Add the vanilla and beat for 3 minutes. Gradually add the sugar and beat on low speed until creamy and of desired consistency.

MAKES ENOUGH FOR ONE 2-LAYER 9-INCH CAKE OR 2 DOZEN CUPCAKES

NOTE: If you are icing a 3-layer cake, use the following recipe proportions:

2 cups (4 sticks) unsalted butter
½ cup milk
12 ounces white chocolate

1 ½ teaspoons vanilla extract
4 cups sifted confectioners' sugar

Seven-Minute Icing

This classic American marshmallow-like frosting is a childhood favorite of many. It is a cooked icing but is relatively simple to make and can be used to frost a wide variety of cakes.

3 egg whites
2¼ cups sugar
½ cup cold water

1½ tablespoons light corn syrup
⅛ teaspoon salt
1½ teaspoons vanilla extract

Combine the egg whites, sugar, water, syrup, and salt in the top of a double boiler and place over rapidly boiling water. On the high speed of an electric mixer, beat constantly for 6–8 minutes, or until the icing stands up in soft peaks. Remove from the heat, add the vanilla, and beat about 1 minute more, or until the icing has the desired spreading consistency. Use immediately.

MAKES ENOUGH FOR ONE 2- OR 3-LAYER 9-INCH CAKE

Lemon Buttercream

A refreshing and fruity icing that complements both lemon and white cakes.

1 cup (2 sticks) unsalted butter,
   very soft
8 cups confectioners' sugar

½ cup fresh lemon juice
1 teaspoon grated lemon zest

Place the butter in a large mixing bowl. Add 4 cups of the sugar and then the juice and the zest. Beat until smooth and creamy. Gradually add the remaining sugar, 1 cup at at time, until icing is thick enough to be of good spreading consistency. If desired, add a few drops of yellow food coloring and mix thoroughly. Use and store at room temperature.

THIS YIELDS ICING FOR ONE 2- OR 3-LAYER 9-INCH CAKE

Caramel Frosting

Allysa loves anything with caramel, and she always wanted to make an easy caramel frosting that didn't involve a candy thermometer. Here it is. (This icing tastes better if made the day before the cake because the brown sugar gives the icing a slightly grainy texture that improves if allowed to set overnight.)

2 cups (4 sticks) unsalted butter, softened
5 cups sifted confectioners' sugar
1 ½ cups firmly packed light brown sugar

½ cup milk
2 tablespoons dark corn syrup
2 teaspoons vanilla extract

In a large bowl, on the medium speed of an electric mixer, cream the butter until smooth. Add the sugars and beat on low speed for 2 minutes. Add the milk, syrup, and vanilla, and beat until smooth and creamy, 3–5 minutes. Use immediately or store, covered, at room temperature for up to 2 days.

MAKES ENOUGH FOR ONE 3-LAYER 9-INCH CAKE OR 3 DOZEN CUPCAKES

Basic Creamy Custard Filling

This is a classic custard. It's fantastic in cakes as a filling or as a dessert accompanied by a simple cookie.

1 cup sugar
6 tablespoons all-purpose flour
¼ teaspoon salt
2 cups milk

4 egg yolks, slightly beaten
1 tablespoon plus 1 teaspoon vanilla
    extract

In a small bowl, combine the sugar, the flour, and the salt. Set aside.

In a heavy-bottomed medium-size saucepan, heat the milk until very hot but not boiling. Remove from heat. Pour the milk into the dry ingredients and beat until well blended. Pour back into pot and stir continuously over low heat for 5 minutes until very thick and smooth. Add the egg yolks and cook for 3 more minutes. Remove from heat and cool for 10 minutes, stirring from time to time. Then add the vanilla. Cover and refrigerate until needed.

THIS YIELDS FILLING FOR ONE 2- OR 3-LAYER 9-INCH CAKE

Butterscotch Cream Cheese Frosting

This not-so-sweet frosting combines a deep butterscotch flavor with the tanginess of the cream cheese. It goes just wonderfully with the apple layer cake.

1 pound (two 8-ounce packages) cream cheese, softened

6 tablespoons unsalted butter, softened

1 cup firmly packed light brown sugar

2 tablespoons dark corn syrup

1 teaspoon vanilla extract

In a large bowl, on the medium speed of an electric mixer, beat the cream cheese and butter until smooth, about 3 minutes. Add the sugar, corn syrup, and vanilla, and beat until smooth and creamy.

Cover and refrigerate frosting for 1 hour to thicken before using.

MAKES ENOUGH FOR ONE 2- OR 3-LAYER 9-INCH CAKE

Chocolate Buttercream

The key to achieving the same creamy texture that we did at the bakery is in beating the icing at the proper speeds for the proper amount of time. If beaten at too high a speed, the icing incorporates a lot of air and becomes fluffy rather than creamy.

1½ cups (3 sticks) unsalted butter, softened
2 tablespoons milk
9 ounces semisweet chocolate, melted and cooled to lukewarm (see Note)

1 teaspoon vanilla extract
2¼ cups sifted confectioners' sugar

NOTE: To melt the chocolate, place in a double boiler over simmering water on low heat for about 5–10 minutes. Stir occasionally until completely smooth and no pieces of chocolate remain. Remove from the heat and let cool for 5–15 minutes, or until lukewarm.

In a large bowl, on the medium speed of an electric mixer, beat the butter until creamy, about 3 minutes. Add the milk carefully and beat until smooth. Add the melted chocolate and beat well, about 2 minutes. Add the vanilla and beat for 3 minutes. Gradually add the sugar and beat on low speed until creamy and of desired consistency.

MAKES ENOUGH FOR ONE 2-LAYER 9-INCH CAKE OR 2 DOZEN CUPCAKES

NOTE: If you are icing a 3-layer cake, use the following recipe proportions:

2 cups (4 sticks) unsalted butter
3 tablespoons milk
12 ounces semisweet chocolate

1½ teaspoons vanilla extract
3 cups confectioners' sugar

White Chocolate
Cream Cheese Icing

White chocolate and cream cheese together in a fabulous icing that's just perfect with the banana layer cake. (It's also really good on the devil's food cupcakes.)

1 pound (two 8-ounce packages) cream cheese, softened

6 tablespoons unsalted butter, softened

1 teaspoon vanilla extract

8 ounces white chocolate (such as Lindt—do not use a baking chocolate like Callebaut), melted and cooled to lukewarm temperature (see Note)

NOTE: To melt the chocolate, place in a double boiler over simmering water on low heat for about 5–10 minutes. Stir occasionally until completely smooth and no pieces of chocolate remain. Remove from heat and let cool for 5–15 minutes, or until lukewarm.

In a large bowl, on the medium speed of an electric mixer, beat together the cream cheese and butter until smooth, about 3 minutes. Add the vanilla and beat well. Add the melted chocolate, and beat well. Use immediately or store, covered, at room temperature for up to 4 hours.

MAKES ENOUGH FOR ONE 2-LAYER 9-INCH CAKE

Lemon Curd Filling

Try this on toast or scones for a sweet breakfast or teatime treat.

12 egg yolks, at room temperature
3 tablespoons grated lemon zest
1 cup fresh lemon juice
½ teaspoon lemon extract

1 ½ cups sugar
1 cup (2 sticks) unsalted butter, cut in
    small pieces

In a medium-size saucepan, whisk the first five ingredients until thoroughly combined. Using a wooden spoon, stir constantly over medium heat. Cook about 20 minutes until thick and bubbly. Remove from heat and add the butter, one piece at a time, stirring to incorporate. Place in refrigerator overnight until firm.

MAKES 3½ CUPS, OR ENOUGH FILLING FOR ONE 2- OR 3-LAYER 9 INCH CAKE

Caramel Sauce

Caramel is not difficult to prepare, but it has to be done correctly. Pay attention as it nears the end of cooking because it can go from deep amber to burnt very, very quickly.

1 cup cold water
3 cups sugar

2 cups heavy cream, at room
   temperature

In a medium-size saucepan, combine the water and sugar. Set over medium-low heat, stirring occasionally, until the sugar dissolves, about 3 minutes, making sure no sugar is sticking to the sides of the pan. Increase the heat to high and boil without stirring until the syrup becomes a deep amber color, about 15 minutes. To prevent the syrup from becoming grainy, use a pastry brush dipped into cold water to brush down any sugar crystals sticking to the sides of the pan. Swirl the pan occasionally for even browning.

Once the syrup turns deep amber in color, immediately remove from the heat. Slowly and carefully add the cream to the syrup (the mixture will bubble vigorously), whisking constantly until the cream is incorporated.

Return the pan to medium-low heat and stir until the sauce is smooth, about 1 minute.

Remove from the heat and allow to come to room temperature before refrigerating. The caramel can be stored for up to 1 month in the refrigerator.

MAKES 3½ CUPS

Sweet Vanilla Whipped Cream

Allysa believes that no pie is complete without a large dollop of whipped cream to accompany it. Since she suggests it so often in her recipes, she thought she should include her version of not-too-sweet whipped cream.

2 cups heavy cream
2 teaspoons sugar

2 teaspoons vanilla extract

Place all the ingredients in a medium-size bowl and whip with an eggbeater or a whisk until soft peaks form. Serve immediately with your favorite dessert, or cover tightly with plastic wrap and refrigerate for up to 4 hours.

MAKES APPROXIMATELY 2 CUPS

Butterscotch Filling

This rich custard has a distinctive caramel flavor. It's especially good with white or yellow cake.

1 cup firmly packed dark brown sugar
4 tablespoons (½ stick) unsalted
   butter
2 cups milk

6 tablespoons all-purpose flour
1 teaspoon salt
4 large eggs, slightly beaten
1 teaspoon vanilla extract

In a heavy-bottomed medium-size saucepan, combine the sugar and the butter, cooking over low heat. Stir constantly until the sugar has melted and the mixture is thoroughly blended. Add 1 cup of the milk, blend well, and continue cooking over low heat. In a small bowl, combine the flour and the salt with the remaining cup of milk and beat until smooth. Add this to the first mixture, stirring or whisking constantly. Continue cooking until thickened. Beat in the eggs and cook another 2 minutes. Remove from heat and cool for 10 minutes, stirring from time to time. Then add the vanilla. Cover and refrigerate until needed.

THIS YIELDS FILLING FOR ONE 2- OR 3-LAYER 9-INCH CAKE

CHEESECAKES
AND
CHEESE PIES

Crumb-Topped Cheesecake

When Allysa was growing up, her dad would rave about a fabulous crumb-topped cheesecake he enjoyed as a child in Brooklyn but had never seen since. After some experimenting, she came up with this recipe, unique in that it's made without a crust (but we believe you'll agree that the confectioners' sugar topping, with a hint of cinnamon, more than makes up for it).

FILLING

2 pounds (4 eight-ounce packages) cream cheese, softened

1 ¼ cups sugar

5 large eggs, at room temperature

2 tablespoons heavy cream

1 tablespoon vanilla extract

TOPPING

2 cups all-purpose flour

2 cups confectioners' sugar

½ teaspoon cinnamon

1 ½ teaspoons baking powder

1 cup (2 sticks) unsalted butter, cut into small pieces

Preheat oven to 325 degrees. Butter the bottom and sides of a 10-inch springform pan.

To make the filling: In a large bowl, on the low speed of an electric mixer, beat the cream cheese until very smooth. Gradually add the sugar. Add the eggs one at a time. To ensure that the batter has no lumps and that no ingredients are stuck to the bottom of the bowl, stop the mixer several times and scrape down the sides of the bowl with a rubber spatula. Stir in the heavy cream and the vanilla extract.

Pour the batter into the prepared pan and set the pan on a baking sheet. Bake for 40 minutes.

Meanwhile, prepare the topping: In a medium-size bowl, mix together the flour, the sugar, the cinnamon, and the baking powder. Using a pastry blender, cut in the butter until the mixture resembles coarse crumbs.

Slowly and carefully remove cheesecake, with baking sheet, to add topping. Sprinkle crumbs evenly over top of cake, return it immediately to oven, and bake for an additional 20 minutes.

(continued)

Bake until edges are set and center moves only slightly when pan is shaken, about 1 hour. At the end of the baking time, turn off the heat, and using a wooden spoon to keep oven door slightly ajar, cool cake in oven for 1 hour before removing. Cover and refrigerate for at least 12 hours.

Remove cake from the refrigerator at least 15–30 minutes before cutting and serving.

MAKES ONE 10-INCH CHEESECAKE

Mocha Rum Cheesecake

The rum, espresso, and chocolaty-creamy filling atop a dark chocolate cookie crust makes this cheesecake pure decadence.

CRUST

4 tablespoons (½ stick) unsalted
   butter, melted
1 ½ cups chocolate wafer crumbs

FILLING

4 tablespoons light rum
1 tablespoon instant espresso
1 pound (2 eight-ounce packages)
   cream cheese, softened

1 cup sugar
3 large eggs, at room temperature
4 ounces semisweet chocolate, melted
   (see Note)
1 ½ teaspoons vanilla extract
3 cups sour cream, at room
   temperature

NOTE: To melt chocolate, place in a double boiler over simmering water on low heat for approximately 5–10 minutes. Stir occasionally until completely smooth, and no pieces of chocolate remain. Remove from heat and let cool for 5–10 minutes.

Preheat oven to 325 degrees.

To make the crust: In a small bowl, combine the butter with the chocolate wafer crumbs. Press into the bottom of a buttered 10-inch springform pan. Bake for 10 minutes. Remove from oven and cool on rack.

To make the filling: In a separate bowl, whisk the rum and the espresso until well blended. Set aside.

In a large bowl, on the low speed of an electric mixer, beat the cream cheese until very smooth. Gradually add the sugar. Add the eggs one at a time. To ensure that the batter has no lumps and that no ingredients are stuck to the bottom of the bowl, stop the mixer several times and scrape down the sides of the bowl with a rubber spatula. Beat in the melted chocolate until smooth. Stir in the vanilla and the rum mixture until well combined. Stir in the sour cream, mixing thoroughly.

(continued)

Pour the batter into the prepared pan and set the pan on a baking sheet. Bake until edges are set and center moves only slightly when pan is shaken, about 80 minutes. At the end of the baking time, turn off the heat, and using a wooden spoon to keep oven door slightly ajar, cool the cake in oven for 1 hour before removing. Cover and refrigerate for at least 12 hours.

Remove cake from the refrigerator at least 15–30 minutes before cutting and serving.

MAKES ONE 10-INCH CHEESECAKE

Strawberry Cream Cheese Pie with Graham Cracker Crust

At the farmers' market near Allysa's house every summer, there is a woman who grows and sells the most perfect half-wild strawberries she has ever eaten. She eats the first pint of the season straight out of the container, and with the second pint she makes this really great cream cheese pie.

CRUST
½ cup (1 stick) unsalted butter, melted
1 ¼ cups graham cracker crumbs
½ cup chopped toasted pecans
   (see Note)
¼ cup unpacked light brown sugar

FILLING
1 pound (two 8-ounce packages)
   cream cheese, softened

1 cup confectioners' sugar
¼ cup sour cream
1 teaspoon vanilla extract

TOPPING
1 pint (2 cups) fresh strawberries,
   sliced in half

NOTE: To toast the pecans, place on a baking sheet in a 350-degree oven for 15 minutes, or until lightly browned and fragrant.

Preheat oven to 350 degrees.

To make the crust: In a medium-size bowl, combine the butter with the graham cracker crumbs, pecans, and sugar. Press firmly into a lightly buttered 9-inch glass pie dish. Place on a baking sheet and bake for 12 minutes. Remove from the oven and allow to cool on a wire rack.

To make the filling: In a large bowl, on the low speed of an electric mixer, beat together the cream cheese and sugar until smooth and creamy. Add the sour cream and vanilla, and continue to beat at low speed until well combined.

Refrigerate the filling while the crust is cooling. When the crust is completely cooled, spread the filling evenly in the crust with a rubber spatula. Arrange the sliced strawberries on top of the filling in a decorative manner.

Refrigerate the pie for at least 8 hours or overnight to ensure that the filling sets.

MAKES ONE 9-INCH PIE

Raspberry Marzipan Cheesecake

Growing up with German grandparents, Jennifer often received marzipan as a treat. It remains one of her favorite sweets to this day and incorporated into this cheesecake makes this a delectable dessert.

CRUST
6 tablespoons (¾ stick) unsalted
   butter, melted
1 ½ cups vanilla wafer crumbs
½ cup finely chopped toasted almonds
   (see Note)

FILLING
1 pound (2 eight-ounce packages)
   cream cheese, softened
8 ounces almond paste, crumbled

1 cup sugar
3 large eggs, at room temperature
1 ½ teaspoons vanilla extract
3 cups sour cream, at room
   temperature

TOPPING
6 tablespoons raspberry preserves
1 teaspoon lemon juice

GARNISH (OPTIONAL)
1 cup fresh raspberries

NOTE: To toast hazelnuts, place on a baking sheet in a 325-degree oven for approximately 10–15 minutes or until lightly browned and fragrant.

Preheat oven to 325 degrees.

To make the crust: In a small bowl, combine the butter with the vanilla wafer crumbs and the almonds. Press into the bottom of a buttered 10-inch springform pan. Bake for 10 minutes. Remove from oven and cool on rack.

To make the filling: In a large bowl, on the low speed of an electric mixer, beat the cream cheese and the almond paste until very smooth. Gradually add the sugar. Add the eggs one at a time. To ensure that the batter has no lumps and that no ingredients are stuck to the bottom of the bowl, stop the mixer several times and scrape down the sides of the bowl with a rubber spatula. Stir in the vanilla and the sour cream until well combined.

To make the topping: Process the raspberry preserves with the lemon juice until smooth.

Pour the batter into the prepared pan and set the pan on a baking sheet. Drop the raspberry mixture by the teaspoonful onto the top of the batter. Using the tip of a sharp knife, swirl the raspberry mixture into batter, forming a decorative pattern.

Bake until edges are set and center moves only slightly when pan is shaken, about 80 minutes. At the end of the baking time, turn off the heat, and using a wooden spoon to keep oven door slightly ajar, cool the cake in oven for 1 hour before removing. Cover and refrigerate for at least 12 hours.

Remove cake from the refrigerator at least 15–30 minutes before cutting and serving.

Garnish with fresh raspberries before cutting and serving, if desired.

MAKES ONE 10-INCH CHEESECAKE

Caramel Pecan Cheesecake

The secret to the success of this cheesecake is the homemade caramel mixed with the nutty flavor of the toasted pecans. At our bakery it was a sure sell-out every time.

CRUST
½ cup (1 stick) unsalted butter, melted
1 ¼ cup vanilla wafer crumbs
½ cup finely chopped pecans

FILLING
2 pounds (4 eight-ounce packages)
    cream cheese, softened
1 ¼ cups sugar

5 large eggs, at room temperature
2 tablespoons heavy cream
1 tablespoon vanilla extract

TOPPING
1 cup cold caramel (or more if
    desired) (recipe on page 140)
1 cup coarsely chopped toasted
    pecans (see Note)

NOTE: To toast pecans, place on a baking sheet in a 325-degree oven for approximately 10–15 minutes or until lightly browned and fragrant.

Preheat oven to 325 degrees.

To make the crust: In a small bowl, combine the butter with the vanilla wafer crumbs and the pecans. Press into the bottom of a buttered 10-inch springform pan. Bake for 10 minutes. Remove from oven and cool on rack.

To make the filling: In a large bowl, on the low speed of an electric mixer, beat the cream cheese until very smooth. Gradually add the sugar. Add the eggs one at a time. To ensure that the batter has no lumps and that no ingredients are stuck to the bottom of the bowl, stop the mixer several times and scrape down the sides of the bowl with a rubber spatula. Stir in the heavy cream and the vanilla.

Pour the batter into the prepared pan and set the pan on a baking sheet. Bake until edges are set and center moves only slightly when pan is shaken, about 1 hour. At the end of the baking time, turn off the heat, and using a wooden spoon to keep oven door slightly ajar, cool cake in oven for 1 hour before removing. Cover and refrigerate for at least 12 hours.

Spoon cold caramel evenly over top of cake. Sprinkle with pecans. Return cake to refrigerator.

Remove cake from the refrigerator at least 15–30 minutes before cutting and serving.

MAKES ONE 10-INCH CHEESECAKE

Chocolate Swirl Cheesecake

For those who like a subtle touch of chocolate, this is the cheesecake for you! This was one of our original cheesecake recipes.

CRUST
5 tablespoons unsalted butter, melted
2 cups chocolate wafer crumbs

FILLING
2 pounds (4 eight-ounce packages)
   cream cheese, softened
1 ¼ cups sugar

5 large eggs, at room temperature
2 tablespoons heavy cream
1 tablespoon vanilla extract

TOPPING
3 tablespoons heavy cream
4 ounces semisweet chocolate, finely
   chopped

Preheat oven to 325 degrees.

To make the crust: In a small bowl, combine the butter with the chocolate wafer crumbs. Press into the bottom of a buttered 10-inch springform pan. Bake for 10 minutes. Remove from oven and cool on rack.

To make the filling: In a large bowl, on the low speed of an electric mixer, beat the cream cheese until very smooth. Gradually add the sugar. Add the eggs one at a time. To ensure that the batter has no lumps and that no ingredients are stuck to the bottom of the bowl, stop the mixer several times, and scrape down the sides of the bowl with a rubber spatula. Stir in the heavy cream and the vanilla.

Pour the batter into the prepared pan and set the pan on a baking sheet.

To prepare the topping: In a small saucepan over high heat, bring the heavy cream to a simmer. Add the chocolate, turning heat down to low and stirring constantly until chocolate is completely melted. Remove from heat and cool slightly. Drop this mixture by the teaspoonful onto top of batter. Using the tip of a sharp knife, swirl chocolate mixture into batter, forming a decorative pattern.

Bake until edges are set and center moves only slightly when pan is shaken, about 1 hour. At the end of the baking time, turn off the heat, and using a wooden spoon to keep oven door slightly ajar, cool cake in oven for 1 hour before removing. Cover and refrigerate for at least 12 hours.

Remove cake from the refrigerator at least 15–30 minutes before cutting and serving.

MAKES ONE 10-INCH CHEESECAKE

Heath Bar Almond Crunch Cheesecake

This unbelievably delicious cheesecake will have toffee lovers clamoring for seconds; now, you can have your cake and candy, too. Allysa, who feels that the addition of Heath Bars to just about any dessert is a good thing, developed this idea one rare quiet evening at the bakery.

CRUST
1 cup all-purpose flour
¼ cup confectioners' sugar
1 cup finely chopped toasted almonds
    (see Note)
½ cup (1 stick) unsalted butter,
    softened, cut into small pieces

FILLING
2 pounds (4 eight-ounce packages)
    cream cheese, softened

1¼ cups sugar
5 large eggs, at room temperature
2 tablespoons heavy cream
1 tablespoon vanilla extract

TOPPING
3 coarsely chopped Heath Bars or
    chocolate-covered toffee bars
    (about ¾ cup)
¾ cup coarsely chopped toasted
    almonds (see Note)

NOTE: To toast almonds, place on a baking sheet in a 325-degree oven for approximately 10–15 minutes or until lightly browned and fragrant.

Preheat oven to 325 degrees.

To make the crust: In a medium-size bowl, combine the flour with the sugar and the almonds. Using a pastry blender, cut in the butter until the mixture resembles coarse crumbs. Press into the bottom of a buttered 10-inch springform pan. Bake for 10 minutes. Remove from oven and cool on rack.

To make the filling: In a large bowl, on the low speed of an electric mixer, beat the cream cheese until very smooth. Gradually add the sugar. Add the eggs one at a time. To ensure that the batter has no lumps and that no ingredients are stuck to the bottom of the bowl, stop the mixer several times and scrape down the sides of the bowl with a rubber spatula. Stir in the heavy cream and the vanilla.

(continued)

Pour the batter into the prepared pan and set the pan on a baking sheet. Bake until edges are set and center moves only slightly when pan is shaken, about 1 hour. At the end of the baking time, remove cheesecake from oven to add topping. Sprinkle Heath Bar pieces and almonds evenly over top of cake and return to oven to cool. Turn off the heat, and using a wooden spoon to keep oven door slightly ajar, cool cake in oven for 1 hour before removing. Cover and refrigerate for at least 12 hours.

Remove cake from the refrigerator at least 15–30 minutes before cutting and serving.

MAKES ONE 10-INCH CHEESECAKE

Cream Cheese Pecan Pie

The surprising combination of the cream cheese filling with the standard pecan pie filling is quite delicious.

CREAM CHEESE FILLING
½ pound (one 8-ounce package)
    cream cheese (not softened)
⅓ cup sugar
1 large egg, at room temperature
1 teaspoon vanilla extract
¼ teaspoon salt

CORN SYRUP FILLING
3 large eggs, at room temperature
1 cup light corn syrup

¼ cup firmly packed light brown sugar
1 teaspoon vanilla extract

CRUST
1 cup plus 2 tablespoons all-purpose
    flour
½ cup solid vegetable shortening
3 tablespoons ice water

1 ¼ cups coarsely chopped toasted
    pecans (see Note)

NOTE: To toast the pecans, place on a baking sheet in a 350-degree oven for 15 minutes, or until lightly browned and fragrant.

Preheat oven to 375 degrees.

To make the cream cheese filling: In a medium-size bowl, on the medium speed of an electric mixer, beat together the cream cheese and sugar until smooth and creamy. Add the egg, vanilla, and salt, continuing to beat until ingredients are well blended and mixture is considerably thicker, 3–5 minutes. (I recommend using the whisk attachment if your mixer has one.) Set aside.

To make the corn syrup filling: In a small bowl, on the medium speed of an electric mixer, beat the eggs for 1 minute. Add the corn syrup, sugar, and vanilla, and beat 1 minute more. Set aside.

To make the crust: Place the flour in a large bowl and, using a pastry blender, cut in the shortening until the pieces are pea-size. Sprinkle the ice water by tablespoonfuls over the flour mixture and toss with a fork until all the dough is moistened. Gather the

(continued)

dough into a ball and roll it out on a lightly floured surface to fit a 9-inch glass pie dish and trim, leaving ½ inch around the edge. Fold the edges under all around the rim and crimp.

Spread the cream cheese filling evenly in the bottom of the crust. Sprinkle with the pecans. Slowly and carefully pour the corn syrup filling over the pecans. Place the pie on a baking sheet and bake for 50–60 minutes, or until the center of the pie is set.

Cool on a wire rack for at least 4 hours before cutting and serving. This pie is best served at room temperature, not warm, with sweetened whipped cream.

MAKES ONE 9-INCH PIE

White Chocolate Hazelnut Cheesecake

Allysa and her cousin Kim brainstormed one Thanksgiving when an uneven oven produced a cheesecake with cracks on the surface. They decided to pile white chocolate and nuts on top to cover up the cracks and created a cake that turned out to be more delicious than the original.

CRUST
½ cup (1 stick) unsalted butter, melted
1 cup graham cracker crumbs
¼ cup sugar
½ cup ground toasted hazelnuts
    (see Note)

FILLING
2 pounds (4 eight-ounce packages)
    cream cheese, softened
1¼ cups sugar

4 large eggs, at room temperature
3 ounces white chocolate, finely
    chopped
3 tablespoons Frangelico liqueur

TOPPING
1 cup coarsely chopped toasted
    hazelnuts (see Note)
1 cup coarsely chopped white
    chocolate

NOTE: To toast hazelnuts, place on a baking sheet in a 325-degree oven for approximately 10–15 minutes or until lightly browned and fragrant.

Preheat oven to 325 degrees.

To make the crust: In a small bowl, combine the butter with the graham cracker crumbs, the sugar, and the hazelnuts. Press into the bottom of a buttered 10-inch springform pan. Bake for 10 minutes. Remove from oven and cool on rack.

To make the filling: In a large bowl, on the low speed of an electric mixer, beat the cream cheese until very smooth. Gradually add the sugar. Add the eggs one at a time. To ensure that the batter has no lumps and that no ingredients are stuck to the bottom of the bowl, stop the mixer several times, and scrape down the sides of the bowl with a rubber spatula. Stir in the white chocolate and the liqueur until well combined.

Pour the batter into the prepared pan and set the pan on a baking sheet. After

(continued)

40 minutes, carefully remove from oven and sprinkle hazelnuts and white chocolate evenly over top of cake. Return immediately to oven and bake an additional 20 minutes, until edges are set and center moves only slightly when pan is shaken. At the end of the baking time, turn off the heat, and using a wooden spoon to keep oven door slightly ajar, cool cake in oven for 1 hour before removing. Cover and refrigerate for at least 12 hours.

Remove cake from the refrigerator at least 15–30 minutes before cutting and serving.

MAKES ONE 10-INCH CHEESECAKE

Caramel Apple Pecan Cheesecake

Every Thanksgiving at Allysa's cousin Polly's house they used to gather the evening before to do the holiday baking, and every year Allysa was called upon to create a new cheesecake. This is a recent year's recipe, and it was loved by all.

CRUST

1 cup cake flour (not self-rising)

¼ cup firmly packed light brown sugar

½ cup (1 stick) unsalted butter, softened and cut into small pieces

1 cup chopped toasted pecans (see Note)

FILLING

2 pounds (four 8-ounce packages) cream cheese, softened

1¼ cups sugar

5 large eggs, at room temperature

2 tablespoons heavy cream

1 tablespoon vanilla extract

APPLE TOPPING

2½ cups thinly sliced tart apples (such as Granny Smith)

¼ cup sugar

⅛ teaspoon cinnamon

1 tablespoon unsalted butter

GARNISH

⅔ cup Caramel Sauce (page 140)

⅓ cup coarsely chopped toasted pecans (see Note)

NOTE: To toast the pecans, place on a baking sheet in a 350-degree oven for 15 minutes, or until lightly browned and fragrant.

Preheat oven to 350 degrees.

To make the crust: In a large bowl, mix together the flour and sugar. Using a pastry blender, cut in the butter until the mixture resembles coarse crumbs. Add the pecans and, using your hands, toss until all the ingredients are well combined. Press into the bottom of a buttered 10-inch springform pan. Bake for 20 minutes.

Remove from the oven and allow to cool on a wire rack. Lower the oven temperature to 325 degrees.

To make the filling: In a large bowl, on the low speed of an electric mixer, beat the cream cheese until very smooth. Gradually add the sugar. Add the eggs, one at a time.

(continued)

To ensure that the batter has no lumps and that no ingredients are stuck to the bottom of the bowl, stop the mixer several times and scrape down the sides of the bowl with a rubber spatula. Stir in the heavy cream and vanilla.

Pour the batter into the prepared pan and set the pan on a baking sheet. Bake until the edges are set and the center moves only slightly when the pan is shaken, about 1 hour. At the end of the baking time, turn off the heat and, using a wooden spoon to keep the oven door slightly ajar, cool the cake in the oven for 1 hour before removing. Cover and refrigerate for at least 12 hours or overnight.

To make the apple topping: Toss the apples with the sugar and cinnamon. In a medium-size saucepan, melt the butter over medium-high heat. Add the apples and cook, stirring occasionally, until the apples are very soft and easily pierced with a fork, 8–10 minutes. Remove the apples from the heat, transfer them to a small bowl, and allow to cool to room temperature, about 45 minutes. When the apples have cooled, spread them evenly in a thin layer over the top of the cheesecake. Return the cake to the refrigerator.

Remove the cake from the refrigerator 15–30 minutes before cutting and serving. To garnish, drizzle the caramel decoratively over the apples and then sprinkle with the pecans.

MAKES ONE 10-INCH CHEESECAKE

Pumpkin Cheesecake with Gingersnap Pecan Crust

This cheesecake is a lovely dessert for an autumn dinner party. Cheesecakes are ideal for entertaining because they can be made one to two days in advance, long before the guests arrive.

CRUST
½ cup (1 stick) unsalted butter, melted
1 ½ cups gingersnap cookie crumbs
½ cup chopped toasted pecans
    (see Note)

FILLING
¾ pound (one and a half 8-ounce
    packages) cream cheese, softened
¾ cup sugar

¾ cup firmly packed brown sugar
5 large eggs, at room temperature
1 ½ cups canned pumpkin puree
¾ cup heavy cream
1 ½ teaspoons cinnamon

GARNISH
Sweet Vanilla Whipped Cream
    (see page 141)
Toasted pecan halves (see Note)

NOTE: To toast the pecans, place on a baking sheet in a 350-degree oven for 15 minutes, or until lightly browned and fragrant.

Preheat oven to 325 degrees.

To make the crust: In a small bowl, combine the butter with the gingersnap cookie crumbs and pecans. Press into the bottom of a buttered 10-inch springform pan. Bake for 10 minutes. Remove from the oven and allow to cool on a wire rack.

To make the filling: In a large bowl, on the low speed of an electric mixer, beat the cream cheese until very smooth. Gradually add the sugars. Add the eggs, one at a time. Add the pumpkin puree and mix until just blended. To ensure that the batter has no lumps and that no ingredients are stuck to the bottom of the bowl, stop the mixer several times and scrape down the sides of the bowl with a rubber spatula. Stir in the heavy cream and cinnamon.

Pour the batter into the prepared pan and set the pan on a baking sheet. Bake until

(continued)

the edges are set and the center moves only slightly when the pan is shaken, about 1 hour. At the end of the baking time, turn off the heat and, using a wooden spoon to keep the oven door slightly ajar, cool the cake in the oven for 1 hour before removing. Cover and refrigerate for at least 12 hours or overnight.

Remove the cake from the refrigerator 15–30 minutes before cutting and serving. Garnish with the sweetened whipped cream and toasted pecan halves.

MAKES ONE 10-INCH CHEESECAKE

Chocolate Almond Cheesecake

With a crunchy chocolate almond crust and topping sandwiching a chocolaty-smooth and creamy filling, this cheesecake is a multitextured masterpiece!

CRUST
6 tablespoons (¾ stick) unsalted butter, melted

1½ cups chocolate-sandwich cookie crumbs

½ cup finely chopped toasted almonds (see second Note)

FILLING
1 pound (2 eight-ounce packages) cream cheese, softened

4 ounces almond paste, crumbled

1 cup sugar

3 large eggs, at room temperature

6 ounces semisweet chocolate, melted (see first Note)

1½ teaspoons vanilla extract

5 tablespoons amaretto-flavored liqueur

3 cups sour cream, at room temperature

TOPPING
½ cup crumbled chocolate-sandwich cookies

½ cup coarsely chopped toasted almonds (see second Note)

NOTES: To melt chocolate, place in a double boiler over simmering water on low heat for approximately 5–10 minutes. Stir occasionally until completely smooth and no pieces of chocolate remain. Remove from heat and let cool for 5–10 minutes.

To toast almonds, place on a baking sheet in a 325-degree oven for approximately 10–15 minutes or until lightly browned and fragrant.

Preheat oven to 325 degrees.

To make the crust: In a small bowl, combine the butter with the chocolate cookie crumbs and the almonds. Press into the bottom of a buttered 10-inch springform pan. Bake for 10 minutes. Remove from oven and cool on rack.

To make the filling: In a large bowl, on the low speed of an electric mixer, beat the

(continued)

cream cheese and the almond paste until very smooth. Gradually add the sugar. Add the eggs one at a time. To ensure that the batter has no lumps and that no ingredients are stuck to the bottom of the bowl, stop the mixer several times and scrape down the sides of the bowl with a rubber spatula. Beat in the melted chocolate until smooth. Stir in the vanilla extract and the liqueur until well combined. Then stir in the sour cream, mixing thoroughly.

Pour the batter into the prepared pan and set the pan on a baking sheet. Bake until edges are set and center moves only slightly when pan is shaken, about 80 minutes. At the end of the baking time, remove cheesecake from oven to add topping. Sprinkle cookie crumbs and almonds evenly over top of cake, and return to oven to cool.

Turn off the heat, and using a wooden spoon to keep oven door slightly ajar, cool the cake in oven for 1 hour before removing. Cover and refrigerate for at least 12 hours.

Remove cake from the refrigerator at least 15–30 minutes before cutting and serving.

MAKES ONE 10-INCH CHEESECAKE

Cheese Pie

When Allysa was growing up, her parents would host card games at their home, and friend Sally Terry would always bring one of her fabulous cheese pies. She finally divulged her secret recipe, and it became a tradition for Allysa and her mom, Geri, to bake these light custardlike pies every Christmas Eve, to be eaten the next day after Christmas dinner. The recipe calls for two pies, because as you will see, one is never enough!

CRUST

12 tablespoons (1 ½ sticks) unsalted
    butter, softened
3 tablespoons sugar
3 large eggs, at room temperature
3 cups all-purpose flour
3 tablespoons baking powder

FILLING

1 pound (2 eight-ounce packages)
    cream cheese, softened

1 cup sugar
2 tablespoons flour
2 ½ cups milk
1 tablespoon vanilla extract
4 large eggs, separated, at room
    temperature (see Note)
Juice of ½ lemon
Cinnamon sugar for sprinkling

NOTE: It is best to separate the eggs when cold and then allow them to come to room temperature before proceeding with the recipe.

Preheat oven to 325 degrees.

To make the crust: In a large bowl, on the low speed of an electric mixer, cream the butter and the sugar until smooth. Add the eggs one at a time and mix well. Add the flour and the baking powder, beating until just combined. Gather the dough into a ball, separate into two pieces, and wrap one piece in waxed paper and set aside. Roll out the dough on a lightly floured surface to fit into a 9-inch glass pie dish and fold the edges under all around the rim and crimp. Repeat with second half of dough in a second pie dish. Place the pie crusts on a jelly roll or cookie sheet.

(continued)

To prepare the filling: In a large bowl, on the low speed of an electric mixer, beat the cream cheese, the sugar, and the flour until smooth and creamy. Add the milk, the vanilla, and the egg yolks, continuing to beat at low speed until well combined. Stir in the lemon juice. In a separate bowl, on the high speed of an electric mixer, beat the egg whites until soft peaks form. Gently fold the egg whites into the filling. Using a a ladle, divide the filling between the prepared pie crusts. Lightly sprinkle with cinnamon sugar.

Bake for 45 minutes, until pies are golden on top and filling is relatively set. Remove from oven and cool for 1 hour at room temperature. Refrigerate overnight before cutting and serving.

MAKES TWO 9-INCH PIES

Coconut Pecan Cheesecake

Coconut and pecans are often paired together, but rarely in a cheesecake. The combination is delectable.

CRUST
½ cup (1 stick) unsalted butter, melted
1 ¼ cups graham cracker crumbs
½ cup chopped toasted pecans
    (see Note)
¼ cup sugar

FILLING
2 pounds (four 8-ounce packages)
    cream cheese, softened
1 cup sugar

5 large eggs, at room temperature
1 ½ cups lightly packed sweetened
    shredded coconut
2 tablespoons heavy cream
2 teaspoons vanilla extract
1 teaspoon coconut extract

GARNISH
½ cup sweetened shredded coconut
¼ cup chopped toasted pecans
    (see Note)

NOTE: To toast the pecans, place on a baking sheet in a 350-degree oven for 15 minutes, or until lightly browned and fragrant.

Preheat oven to 325 degrees.

To make the crust: In a small bowl, combine the butter with the graham cracker crumbs, pecans, and sugar. Press into the bottom of a buttered 10-inch springform pan. Bake for 10 minutes. Remove from the oven and allow to cool on a wire rack.

To make the filling: In a large bowl, on the low speed of an electric mixer, beat the cream cheese until very smooth. Gradually add the sugar. Add the eggs, one at a time. To ensure that the batter has no lumps and that no ingredients are stuck to the bottom of the bowl, stop the mixer several times and scrape down the sides of the bowl with a rubber spatula. Stir in the coconut, heavy cream, and vanilla and coconut extracts.

Pour the batter into the prepared pan and set the pan on a baking sheet. Bake until the edges are set and the center moves only slightly when the pan is shaken, about

(continued)

1 hour. At the end of the baking time, turn off the heat and, using a wooden spoon to keep the oven door slightly ajar, cool the cake in the oven for 1 hour before removing. Cover and refrigerate for at least 12 hours or overnight.

Remove the cake from the refrigerator 15–30 minutes before cutting and serving. To garnish, sprinkle the additional coconut and pecans around the top edge of the cake.

MAKES ONE 10-INCH CHEESECAKE

Peaches and Cream Pie
with Sugar Cookie Crust

This is a lovely, light summertime dessert that you should make only when you have peaches that are perfectly ripe and sweet.

CRUST
½ cup (1 stick) unsalted butter, softened
3 tablespoons sugar
1 large egg yolk, at room temperature
3 tablespoons heavy cream
1 ½ cups all-purpose flour
¼ teaspoon salt

FILLING
1 pound (two 8-ounce packages) cream cheese, softened

1 ½ cups confectioners' sugar
½ cup heavy cream
2 teaspoons vanilla extract

TOPPING
2 ½ cups thinly sliced ripe peaches (see Note)

NOTE: Be sure to blanch the peaches in boiling water for 60 seconds, transfer to an ice water bath, and remove the skins before slicing.

Preheat oven to 375 degrees.

To make the crust: In a large bowl, on the low speed of an electric mixer, cream the butter and sugar until smooth. Add the egg yolk and cream, and mix well. Add the flour and salt, and beat until just combined. Gather the dough into a ball and roll it out on a lightly floured surface to fit into a 9-inch glass pie dish. Fold the edges under all around the rim and crimp. Prick the bottom and sides all over with the tines of a fork. Cover the edge of the pie crust with aluminum foil, place on a baking sheet, and bake for 10 minutes. Carefully remove the foil and continue baking 20 minutes more, until the crust is crisp and golden. Remove from the oven and allow to cool on a wire rack.

To make the filling: In a large bowl, on the low speed of an electric mixer, beat to-

(continued)

gether the cream cheese and sugar until smooth and creamy. Add the heavy cream and vanilla, and continue to beat at low speed until well combined.

Refrigerate the filling while the crust is cooling. When the crust is completely cooled, spread the filling evenly in the crust with a rubber spatula. Arrange the sliced peaches on top of the filling in a decorative manner.

Refrigerate the pie for at least 8 hours or overnight to ensure that the filling sets.

MAKES ONE 9-INCH PIE

PIES, TARTS, AND A COBBLER

Apple Crumb Pie

After much experimenting with crusts, crumbs, and apples, Allysa came up with this recipe as a teenager and has been making it for her family ever since.

CRUST
1 ⅓ cups all-purpose flour
½ cup solid vegetable shortening
3 tablespoons ice water

FILLING
3 tablespoons sugar
1 tablespoon all-purpose flour
⅛ teaspoon cinnamon

3 cups peeled, cored, and sliced tart
    apples, such as Granny Smith

CRUMB TOPPING
2 ¼ cups all-purpose flour
1 ½ cups light brown sugar, unpacked
1 cup (2 sticks) unsalted butter,
    softened, cut into small pieces

Preheat oven to 425 degrees.

To make the crust: Place the flour in a large bowl and, using a pastry blender, cut in the shortening until pieces are pea-size. Sprinkle the ice water by tablespoons over the flour mixture, tossing with a fork until all the dough is moistened. Form dough into a ball. On a lightly floured surface, roll out the dough to fit into a 9-inch glass pie dish. Fold the edges under all around the rim and crimp.

To prepare the filling: In a large bowl, combine the sugar, the flour, and the cinnamon. Add the apple slices and toss gently until coated. Transfer the apple mixture into the pie crust.

To prepare the topping: In a medium-size bowl, mix together the flour and the brown sugar. Using a pastry blender, cut in the butter until the mixture resembles coarse crumbs.

Sprinkle the crumb topping over the apple mixture until well covered. Bake at 425 degrees for 10 minutes, then turn down the oven to 375 degrees and continue baking for an additional 25–35 minutes or until golden brown on top. Serve warm with sweetened whipped cream, if desired.

MAKES ONE 9-INCH PIE

Plum Tart with Almond Streusel Topping

Allysa had never really given much thought to baking with plums until her friend Kate had her over for dinner one evening and served a plum galette for dessert. Allysa went right out to the market, got some plums, and started experimenting. Be sure to use ripe, flavorful plums for this tart.

STREUSEL TOPPING
¾ cup all-purpose flour
¾ cup sugar
6 tablespoons unsalted butter,
    softened and cut into small pieces
½ cup chopped toasted almonds
    (see Note)

FILLING
3 cups thinly sliced plums
¼ cup sugar

1 tablespoon flour
1 teaspoon vanilla extract

CRUST
6 tablespoons unsalted butter,
    softened
2 tablespoons sugar
1 large egg, at room temperature
1 large egg yolk, at room temperature
1½ cups all-purpose flour
1 tablespoon baking powder

NOTE: To toast the almonds, place on a baking sheet in a 350-degree oven for 15 minutes, or until lightly browned and fragrant.

Preheat oven to 325 degrees.

To make the topping: In a medium-size bowl, mix together the flour and sugar. Using a pastry blender, cut in the butter until the mixture resembles coarse crumbs. Add the almonds and, using your hands, toss until all the ingredients are well combined. Set aside.

To make the filling: Place all the ingredients in a large bowl and toss gently until the fruit is evenly coated. Set aside.

To make the crust: In a large bowl, on the low speed of an electric mixer, cream the butter and sugar until smooth. Add the egg and egg yolk, and mix well. Add the flour and baking powder, and beat until just combined. Gather the dough into a ball and roll it out on a lightly floured surface to fit a 10-inch tart pan. Fit the dough into the pan and trim the edge flush with the rim of the pan.

Transfer the fruit filling into the crust and sprinkle the streusel topping evenly over the fruit. Place the tart on a baking sheet and bake for 45 minutes.

Cool on a wire rack for 1–2 hours. Serve warm or at room temperature with sweetened whipped cream, if desired.

MAKES ONE 10-INCH TART

Nancy's Prize-winning Blueberry Pie

This recipe comes from Nancy Schatz of Augusta, Maine. The pie won first prize in the 1991 Old Hallowell Day bake-off.

CRUST
2½ cups all-purpose flour
3 tablespoons sugar
1 teaspoon salt
4 tablespoons (½ stick) unsalted
    butter, chilled and cut into small
    pieces
3 tablespoons solid vegetable
    shortening, chilled and cut into
    small pieces
5 tablespoons orange juice
    (use a variety without pulp)

FILLING
3 cups fresh blueberries
1 cup sugar
3 tablespoons quick-cooking minute
    tapioca
3 tablespoons brandy
2 tablespoons freshly squeezed lemon
    juice
¼ teaspoon cinnamon
2 tablespoons unsalted butter, chilled
    and cut into small pieces

To make the crust: Place the flour, sugar, and salt in a large bowl. Using a pastry blender, cut in the butter and shortening until the pieces are pea-size. Sprinkle the orange juice by tablespoonfuls over the flour mixture and toss with a fork until all the dough is moistened. Gather the dough into a ball and separate into two pieces. Wrap the pieces tightly with plastic wrap and refrigerate for 30 minutes. Five minutes before removing the chilled pie dough from the refrigerator, prepare your filling.

To make the filling: In a large bowl, place the berries, sugar, tapioca, brandy, lemon juice, and cinnamon. Toss gently until the fruit is evenly coated. Let stand for 15 minutes while rolling out the crust.

Preheat oven to 425 degrees.

On a lightly floured surface, roll out half of the dough to fit a 9-inch glass pie dish and trim, leaving ½ inch around the edge. Transfer the fruit filling into the bottom crust, mounding it in the center. Dot with the butter.

Roll out the top crust and trim it to fit, folding the ½-inch excess on the bottom crust over the top edge. Seal by crimping the edges together. Make several 1-inch steam slits in the center of the pie with the tip of a paring knife. Place the pie on a baking sheet and bake for 15 minutes. Lower the oven temperature to 350 degrees and continue baking for an additional 30 minutes.

Cool on a wire rack for at least 2 hours before serving.

MAKES ONE 9-INCH PIE

Apple Tart with
Hazelnut Brown Sugar Topping

This tart is a nice alternative to apple pie, and it makes a great dessert for a dinner party, especially if served with vanilla ice cream and perhaps some caramel sauce.

BROWN SUGAR TOPPING
¾ cup all-purpose flour
½ cup firmly packed light brown sugar
6 tablespoons unsalted butter, softened and cut into small pieces
½ cup coarsely chopped hazelnuts

FILLING
3 cups thinly sliced tart apples
⅓ cup sugar

1 tablespoon flour
1 teaspoon vanilla extract

CRUST
6 tablespoons unsalted butter, softened
2 tablespoons sugar
1 large egg, at room temperature
1 large egg yolk, at room temperature
1½ cups all-purpose flour
1 tablespoon baking powder

Preheat oven to 325 degrees.

To make the topping: In a medium-size bowl, mix together the flour and sugar. Using a pastry blender, cut in the butter until the mixture resembles coarse crumbs. Add the hazelnuts and, using your hands, toss until all the ingredients are well combined. Set aside.

To make the filling: Place all the ingredients in a large bowl and toss gently until the fruit is evenly coated. Set aside.

To make the crust: In a large bowl, on the low speed of an electric mixer, cream the butter and sugar until smooth. Add the egg and egg yolk, and mix well. Add the flour and baking powder, and beat until just combined. Gather the dough into a ball and on a lightly floured surface, roll it out to fit a 10-inch tart pan. Fit the dough into the pan and trim the edge flush with the rim of the pan.

Transfer the fruit filling into the crust and sprinkle the brown sugar topping evenly over the fruit. Place the tart on a baking sheet and bake for 50 minutes.

Cool on a wire rack for 1–2 hours. Serve warm or at room temperature.

MAKES ONE 10-INCH TART

Pecan Pie

We tried many pecan pie recipes when we first opened the bakery. Fellow baker Kathryn McCann brought us this recipe from her Texan grandma, and it was the hands-down winner.

CRUST
1 ⅓ cups all-purpose flour
½ cup solid vegetable shortening
3 tablespoons ice water

FILLING
⅓ cup (5 ⅓ tablespoons) unsalted
   butter, very soft

¾ cup firmly packed light brown sugar
3 large eggs, at room temperature
1 cup light corn syrup
1 teaspoon vanilla extract
⅛ teaspoon salt
1 ½ cups coarsely chopped pecans

Preheat oven to 375 degrees.

To make the crust: Place the flour in a large bowl and, using a pastry blender, cut in the shortening until pieces are pea-size. Sprinkle the ice water by tablespoons over the flour mixture, tossing with a fork until all the dough is moistened. Form dough into a ball. On a lightly floured surface, roll out the dough to fit into a 9-inch glass pie dish. Fold the edges under all around the rim and crimp.

To prepare the filling: In a medium-size bowl, cream the butter and the sugar. Add the remaining ingredients, except for the pecans, in order, one at a time, beating well with each addition. Stir in half the pecans. Carefully pour filling into the prepared crust. Sprinkle the remaining pecans evenly over the filling. Bake for approximately 50–60 minutes or until filling is fairly set. (Filling will firm up as it cools.)

Allow pie to cool for 2 hours before cutting and serving. Serve with sweetened whipped cream if desired.

MAKES ONE 9-INCH PIE

Nectarine Cobbler

A lovely, not-too-sweet summer dessert that's equally delicious with peaches. Be sure to use only the ripest in-season fruit, and serve it warm, with a scoop of vanilla ice cream or a dollop of sweetened whipped cream.

TOPPING
1 cup all-purpose flour
½ cup sugar
1 ½ teaspoons baking powder
½ cup milk
4 tablespoons (½ stick) unsalted
    butter, softened

FILLING
4 cups sliced nectarines
½ cup cold water

⅓ cup unpacked light brown sugar
1 tablespoon cornstarch
1 tablespoon unsalted butter

GARNISH
Cinnamon sugar for sprinkling

Preheat oven to 350 degrees.

To prepare the topping: In a medium-size bowl, stir together the flour, the sugar, and the baking powder. Add the milk and the butter and beat until smooth.

To prepare the filling: In a large saucepan, combine all the ingredients. Cook, stirring often, over medium heat until mixture is thickened and bubbly, about 10 minutes. Pour into an ungreased 8 x 8-inch glass baking dish. Spoon the topping over the filling and spread carefully and evenly with a rubber spatula. Sprinkle with cinnamon sugar. Bake 30–40 minutes or until topping is lightly golden and a cake tester inserted into the center of topping comes out clean.

MAKES ONE 8 x 8-INCH COBBLER

Jill's Apple Pie

This is Allysa's friend Jill Rowe's favorite apple pie recipe. It was the most popular dessert that she made when she owned and ran a local restaurant, The Kitchen, near Allysa's home in upstate New York.

CRUST

2 cups all-purpose flour
½ teaspoon salt
⅔ cup solid vegetable shortening, chilled and cut into small pieces
4 tablespoons (½ stick) unsalted butter, chilled and cut into small pieces
5 tablespoons ice water

FILLING

¾ cup sugar
2 tablespoons all-purpose flour
½ teaspoon cinnamon
⅛ teaspoon nutmeg
⅛ teaspoon salt
6 cups sliced tart green apples (preferably Granny Smith)
4 tablespoons (½ stick) unsalted butter, chilled and cut into small pieces

To make the crust: Place the flour and salt in a large bowl and, using a pastry blender, cut in the shortening and butter until the pieces are pea-size. Sprinkle the ice water by tablespoonfuls over the flour mixture and toss with a fork until all the dough is moistened. Gather the dough into a ball and separate into two pieces. Wrap the pieces tightly with plastic wrap and refrigerate for 30 minutes.

Preheat oven to 400 degrees.

To make the filling: Place the sugar, flour, cinnamon, nutmeg, and salt in a large bowl. Add the apples and toss gently until the fruit is evenly coated.

Roll out one piece of the dough on a lightly floured surface to fit a 9-inch glass pie dish and trim, leaving ½ inch around the edge. Transfer the fruit filling into the bottom crust, mounding it in the center. Dot with the butter.

Roll out the second piece of dough into a top crust and trim to fit. Fold the ½-inch

(continued)

excess on the bottom crust over the top edge. Seal by crimping the edges together. Make several 1-inch steam slits in the center of the pie with the tip of a paring knife. Place the pie on a baking sheet and bake for 50 minutes.

Cool on a wire rack for at least 2 hours. Serve warm or at room temperature with sweetened whipped cream, if desired.

MAKES ONE 9-INCH PIE

Lime Pie with Gingersnap Crust

This pie is as refreshing as it is unbelievably simple. We liked to use "plain ol' limes" for ours, as Key limes are not easily available throughout the year. Fellow baker Ailie Alexander came up with the cookie crust that we think makes the perfect companion to our zingy filling.

CRUST
4 tablespoons (½ stick) unsalted
    butter, melted
1½ cups gingersnap cookie crumbs

FILLING
1½ fourteen-ounce cans sweetened
    condensed milk

6 egg yolks
1 cup fresh lime juice
    (more if desired)
1 tablespoon grated lime zest

Preheat oven to 325 degrees.

To make the crust: In a small bowl, combine the butter and the cookie crumbs. Press firmly into a 9-inch glass pie dish. Bake for 10 minutes. Remove from oven and cool on rack for 10 minutes.

To make the filling: In a medium-size bowl, on the low speed of an electric mixer, beat the milk, the yolks, and the lime juice. Taste to see if the mixture is tart enough. Add more lime juice if desired. Add the zest and incorporate. Carefully pour filling into the prepared crust. Bake for 25–30 minutes, or until the middle has set nicely.

Allow to cool for 20 minutes. Refrigerate for at least 2 hours before cutting and serving.

MAKES ONE 9-INCH PIE

Pumpkin Pie

We all have our favorite pumpkin pie recipe. Here's a good candidate—not too spicy and with a hint of bourbon.

CRUST
1 cup plus 2 tablespoons all-purpose
    flour
½ cup solid vegetable shortening
3 tablespoons ice water

FILLING
One 15-ounce can pumpkin puree
2 large eggs, at room temperature

½ cup sugar
¼ cup firmly packed light brown sugar
1 teaspoon cinnamon
½ teaspoon allspice
¼ teaspoon salt
1 ¼ cups evaporated milk
3 tablespoons bourbon

Preheat oven to 425 degrees.

To make the crust: Place the flour in a large bowl and, using a pastry blender, cut in the shortening until the pieces are pea-size. Sprinkle the ice water by tablespoonfuls over the flour mixture and toss with a fork until all the dough is moistened. Gather the dough into a ball, roll out on a lightly floured surface to fit a 9-inch glass pie dish and trim, leaving ½ inch around the edge. Fold the edges under all around the rim and crimp. Set aside.

To make the filling: In a large bowl, on the medium speed of an electric mixer, combine the pumpkin and eggs, and beat well. Add the sugars, cinnamon, allspice, and salt, and mix until well combined. Combine the evaporated milk and bourbon, and stir into the pumpkin mixture in three parts.

Pour the filling into the prepared crust. Place the pie on a baking sheet and bake for 15 minutes. Lower the oven temperature to 350 degrees and continue baking for an additional 50–60 minutes, or until a tester inserted in the center of the pie comes out clean.

Cool on a wire rack for at least 2 hours. Serve warm or at room temperature with sweetened whipped cream, if desired.

MAKES ONE 9-INCH PIE

Chocolate Pudding Pie

Here's a made-from-scratch pie that's equally good with a graham cracker crust or a butter-based pastry crust, such as the crust from our Sweet Potato Pie (page 192).

CRUST
½ cup (1 stick) unsalted butter, melted
2 cups graham cracker crumbs
2 tablespoons sugar

FILLING
1 ⅓ cups sugar
½ cup unsweetened cocoa powder
⅓ cup cornstarch
⅛ teaspoon salt
4 cups milk
1 ounce semisweet chocolate, finely chopped
1 tablespoon plus 1 teaspoon vanilla extract

Preheat oven to 350 degrees.

To make the crust: In a small bowl, combine the butter with the graham cracker crumbs and the sugar. Press firmly into a lightly buttered 9-inch glass pie dish. Place on a baking sheet and bake for 10 minutes.

Remove from oven and allow to cool on rack.

Meanwhile, prepare the pudding: In a medium-size saucepan, mix the sugar, the cocoa powder, the cornstarch, and the salt. Add half the milk and whisk until the mixture is smooth. Add the remaining milk and continue whisking, over medium heat, until pudding thickens and comes to a boil, about 10 minutes.

Remove from heat and add the chocolate and the vanilla, stirring until chocolate melts completely. Pour immediately into prepared crust. Cool for 20 minutes on wire rack and then refrigerate uncovered for at least 2 hours until chilled. Serve with sweetened whipped cream if desired.

MAKES ONE 9-INCH PIE

Strawberry Double-Crust Pie

A few summers ago Allysa was searching for a good strawberry pie recipe and realized that all the recipes she could find called for a prebaked pie shell, a filling made on top of the stove, and then a chilling period in the refrigerator. She really wanted to make a regular double-crusted, bake-in-the-oven strawberry pie—and with the right amount of tapioca to balance the juiciness of the berries, you can.

FILLING

5 cups fresh strawberries, sliced in half
½ cup sugar
¼ cup quick-cooking minute tapioca
1 teaspoon vanilla extract

CRUST

2⅓ cups all-purpose flour
1 cup solid vegetable shortening,
   cut into small pieces
6 tablespoons ice water

GLAZE

1 tablespoon milk
1 tablespoon sugar

Preheat oven to 400 degrees.

To make the filling: Place all the ingredients in a large bowl and toss gently until the fruit is evenly coated. Let stand for 15 minutes while preparing the crust.

To make the crust: Place the flour in a large bowl and, using a pastry blender, cut in the shortening until the pieces are pea-size. Sprinkle the ice water by tablespoonfuls over the flour mixture and toss with a fork until all the dough is moistened. Gather the dough into a ball, separate into two pieces, and wrap one piece in waxed paper and set aside. Roll out the first piece on a lightly floured surface to fit a 9-inch glass pie dish and trim, leaving ½ inch around the edge.

Transfer the fruit filling into the bottom crust. Unwrap the reserved piece of dough, roll it out as the top crust, and trim to fit. Fold the ½-inch excess on the bottom crust over the top edge. Seal by crimping the edges together. Brush the top crust with the milk, then sprinkle evenly with the sugar. Make several 1-inch steam slits in the center of the pie with the tip of a paring knife. Place the pie on a baking sheet, lower the oven temperature to 350 degrees, and bake for 60–70 minutes, until the crust is golden.

Cool on a wire rack for at least 2 hours. Serve warm or at room temperature, with sweetened whipped cream, if desired.

MAKES ONE 9-INCH PIE

Blueberry Crumb Pie

There's nothing better for dessert at a summer gathering than blueberry pie. We're always asked to bring one whenever invited to a barbecue or picnic. Try this recipe with your favorite berry, or better yet, do a mix!

CRUST
1 ⅓ cups all-purpose flour
½ cup solid vegetable shortening
3 tablespoons ice water

FILLING
½ cup sugar
1 ½ tablespoons cornstarch

2 pints fresh
  blueberries

CRUMB TOPPING
2 ¼ cups all-purpose flour
1 ½ cups unpacked light brown sugar
1 cup (2 sticks) unsalted butter,
  softened, cut into small pieces

Preheat oven to 425 degrees.

To make the crust: Place the flour in a large bowl and, using a pastry blender, cut in the shortening until pieces are pea-size. Sprinkle the ice water by tablespoons over the flour mixture, tossing with a fork until all the dough is moistened. Form dough into a ball. On a lightly floured surface, roll out the dough to fit into a 9-inch glass pie dish. Fold the edges under all around the rim and crimp.

To prepare the filling: In a large bowl, combine the sugar and the cornstarch. Add the berries and toss gently until coated. Transfer the berry mixture into the pie crust.

To prepare the topping: In a medium-size bowl, mix the flour and the brown sugar. Using a pastry blender, cut in the butter until the mixture resembles coarse crumbs.

Sprinkle the crumb topping over the berry mixture until well covered. Bake at 425 degrees for 10 minutes, then turn down the oven to 375 degrees and continue baking for an additional 25–35 minutes or until golden brown on top. Serve warm with a scoop of your favorite vanilla ice cream, if desired.

MAKES ONE 9-INCH PIE

Aunt Daisy's Fresh Fruit Torte

Here's a quick and easy confection that lends itself to any fruit combination you might desire. We decided to use pears and cranberries for a delicious autumn torte.

½ cup (1 stick) unsalted butter, softened
1 cup sugar
2 large eggs, at room temperature
1 cup all-purpose flour
1 teaspoon baking powder

1 teaspoon vanilla extract
1 Bosc pear, thinly sliced (about 1 cup)
½ cup cranberries, coarsely chopped
1 tablespoon cinnamon sugar

Preheat oven to 350 degrees.

Grease and lightly flour one 9 x 2-inch round cake pan, then line the bottom with waxed paper.

In a large bowl, on the low speed of an electric mixer, cream the butter and the sugar until fluffy, about 3 minutes. Add the eggs one at a time, beating well after each addition. Add the flour, the baking powder, and the vanilla until well incorporated. Pour the batter into prepared pan. Spread the pear slices and the berries evenly over the batter. Sprinkle with cinnamon sugar. Bake for about 1 hour until golden brown. Serve warm with a dollop of whipped cream, if desired.

MAKES ONE 9-INCH TORTE

Sweet Potato Pie

Here's a southern favorite that our customers clamored for, particularly around Thanksgiving. Jennifer added a few twists of her own to this durable standard to make it a delectable treat any time.

CRUST

1½ cups all-purpose flour
1 tablespoon sugar
¼ teaspoon salt
8 tablespoons (1 stick) cold unsalted
    butter, cut into small pieces
2–3 tablespoons ice water

FILLING

4 tablespoons (½ stick) unsalted
    butter, softened
¼ cup sugar

¼ cup firmly packed light brown sugar
1½ cups mashed sweet potato, fresh
    or canned, well drained
2 large eggs, at room temperature
½ cup milk
2 tablespoons bourbon
1 tablespoon vanilla extract
¾ teaspoon cinnamon
¼ teaspoon nutmeg
¼ teaspoon ginger
1 teaspoon salt

Preheat oven to 400 degrees.

To make the crust: In a large bowl, place the flour, the sugar, and the salt and, using a pastry blender, cut in the butter until pieces are pea-size. Sprinkle the ice water by tablespoons over the flour mixture, tossing with a fork until all the dough is moistened. Form dough into a ball. On a lightly floured surface, roll out the dough to fit into a 9-inch glass pie dish. Fold the edges under all around the rim and crimp.

Cover the shell with foil and line the foil with pie weights. Bake for 10 minutes. Remove from oven and carefully take out the weights and the foil. Cool on wire rack. Turn oven down to 350 degrees.

To prepare the filling: In a medium-size bowl, on the low speed of an electric mixer, cream the butter and the sugars until fluffy, about 3 minutes. Add the sweet potato, the eggs, the milk, and the bourbon and beat until well combined. Add the vanilla, the spices, and the salt and mix well. Pour the filling into the prepared crust and bake for 45–55 minutes, until filling is fairly set or until a cake tester inserted into center of pie comes out clean.

Allow pie to cool for 30 minutes before serving.

MAKES ONE 9-INCH PIE

Nectarine Double-Crust Pie

No one ever seems to make nectarine pie, and Allysa's not sure why. She adores nectarines (possibly even more than peaches), and this is one of her favorite summertime desserts to make when nectarines are perfectly ripe and in season.

FILLING

5 cups sliced ripe nectarines
(see Note)
½ cup sugar
¼ cup firmly packed light brown
sugar
¼ cup quick-cooking minute tapioca
1 teaspoon vanilla extract

CRUST

2⅓ cups all-purpose flour
1 cup solid vegetable shortening,
cut into small pieces
6 tablespoons ice water

GLAZE

1 tablespoon milk
1 tablespoon sugar

NOTE: Be sure to blanch the nectarines in boiling water for 60 seconds, transfer to an ice water bath, and remove the skins before slicing.

Preheat oven to 400 degrees.

To make the filling: Place all the ingredients in a large bowl and toss gently until the fruit is evenly coated. Let stand for 15 minutes while preparing the crust.

To make the crust: Place the flour in a large bowl and, using a pastry blender, cut in the shortening until the pieces are pea-size. Sprinkle the ice water by tablespoonfuls over the flour mixture and toss with a fork until all the dough is moistened. Gather the dough into a ball, separate into two pieces. Wrap one piece in waxed paper and set aside. Roll out the first piece on a lightly floured surface to fit a 9-inch glass pie dish and trim, leaving ½ inch around the edge.

Transfer the fruit filling into the bottom crust. Unwrap the reserved piece of dough, roll it out as the top crust, and trim to fit. Fold the ½-inch excess on the bottom crust over the top edge. Seal by crimping the edges together. Brush the top crust with the milk, then sprinkle evenly with the sugar. Make several 1-inch steam slits in the center of the pie with the tip of a paring knife. Place the pie on a baking sheet, lower the oven temperature to 350 degrees, and bake for 60–70 minutes, until the crust is golden.

Cool on a wire rack for at least 2 hours. Serve warm or at room temperature with sweetened whipped cream, if desired.

MAKES ONE 9-INCH PIE

Chocolate Pecan Pudding Pie

Allysa has this wonderful childhood memory of a pie that had a custardy chocolate filling with pecans that wasn't like the standard chocolate pecan pie, which she usually finds too rich and sweet. This recipe combines our chocolate pudding from the bakery with pecans and a pastry crust—a simple old-fashioned dessert that comes pretty close to her memory.

CRUST
1 cup plus 2 tablespoons all-purpose
    flour
½ cup solid vegetable shortening
3 tablespoons ice water

FILLING
1 cup sugar
6 tablespoons unsweetened cocoa
    (do not use Dutch process!)

¼ cup cornstarch
Pinch of salt
3 cups milk
1½ cups coarsely chopped toasted
    pecans (see Note)
1 tablespoon vanilla extract

GARNISH
Sweetened whipped cream
Coarsely chopped toasted pecans

NOTE: To toast the pecans, place on a baking sheet in a 350-degree oven for 15 minutes, or until lightly browned and fragrant.

Preheat oven to 425 degrees.

To make the crust: Place the flour in a large bowl and, using a pastry blender, cut in the shortening until the pieces are pea-size. Sprinkle the ice water by tablespoonfuls over the flour mixture and toss with a fork until all the dough is moistened. Gather the dough into a ball and roll out on a lightly floured surface to fit a 9-inch glass pie dish and trim, leaving ½ inch around the edge. Fold the edges under all around the rim and crimp. Prick all over the bottom and sides of the crust with a fork. Place the crust on a baking sheet and bake for 20–25 minutes or until the edges are lightly golden. Remove from the oven and allow to cool to room temperature, about 45 minutes.

To make the filling: In a medium-size saucepan, combine the sugar, cocoa, cornstarch, and salt. Add the milk and whisk over medium heat until the pudding thickens and begins to bubble, about 15 minutes. Remove from the heat and stir in the pecans and vanilla. Pour immediately into the cooled crust. Cover the top of the pie with waxed paper to prevent a skin from forming and cool for 30 minutes.

Remove the waxed paper, cover the pie tightly with plastic wrap, and refrigerate for at least 3 hours or overnight. Serve with sweetened whipped cream, and then garnish with the pecans.

MAKES ONE 9-INCH PIE

ICE CREAMS AND ICEBOX DESSERTS

White Chocolate
Peanut Brittle Ice Cream

This was the most popular ice cream flavor both at the bakery and in grocery stores when Allysa launched her ice cream line in 2001. The peanut brittle complements the brown-sugar-based custard perfectly.

3 large egg yolks, at room temperature
2 cups half-and-half
⅔ cup firmly packed light brown sugar
3 tablespoons light corn syrup
1 tablespoon vanilla extract

1¼ cups coarsely chopped peanut bars
   (preferably Planters)
½ cup coarsely chopped white
   chocolate (preferably Lindt)

In a medium-size bowl, with an eggbeater or a whisk, beat the egg yolks until creamy, 2–3 minutes. Set aside.

In a medium saucepan, combine the half-and-half, sugar, and corn syrup, and cook over medium heat, stirring constantly, until the sugar is completely dissolved. Remove from the heat and add ½ cup of the cream mixture to the egg yolks, stirring to warm the egg yolks. Return the entire mixture to the pot and continue to cook, stirring constantly, until it coats the back of the spoon, about 10 minutes. Remove from the heat and place the pot in a bowl of cold water. When the custard has cooled to room temperature, stir in the vanilla. Cover and refrigerate until completely chilled, preferably overnight.

Pour into an ice cream machine and freeze until partially set, about 20 minutes. Stir in the chopped peanut bars and white chocolate, and continue freezing until firm, following the manufacturer's instructions.

MAKES 1 QUART

Caramel Toffee Pecan Icebox Pie

A brown sugar shortbread crust, a creamy caramel filling, and a topping of Heath bars and toasted pecans—what else could one want in an icebox dessert?

CRUST
⅔ cup all-purpose flour
⅓ cup firmly packed light brown sugar
⅔ cup chopped toasted pecans
  (see Note)
6 tablespoons (¾ stick) unsalted
  butter, softened and cut into small
  pieces

FILLING
12 ounces vanilla caramels
3 tablespoons heavy cream

¾ pound (one and a half 8-ounce
  packages) cream cheese, softened
¾ cup heavy cream, whipped to stiff
  peaks

GARNISH
⅓ cup chopped Heath Bars (or any
  chocolate-covered toffee bars)
⅓ cup chopped toasted pecans
  (see Note)

NOTE: To toast the pecans, place on a baking sheet in a 350-degree oven for 15 minutes, or until lightly browned and fragrant.

Preheat oven to 325 degrees.

To make the crust: In a medium-size bowl, combine the flour, sugar, and pecans. Using a pastry blender, cut in the butter until the mixture resembles coarse crumbs. Press into the bottom of a 9-inch pie dish. Bake for 12–15 minutes, or until lightly golden. Remove from the oven and allow to cool to room temperature, about 45 minutes.

To make the filling: In a medium-size saucepan over low heat, melt the caramels with the 3 tablespoons of cream, stirring occasionally until smooth. Remove from the heat and allow to cool to room temperature, about 30 minutes.

In a large bowl, on the medium speed of an electric mixer, beat the cream cheese until smooth. Add the cooled caramel and beat well.

In a separate bowl, beat the ¾ cup of heavy cream until stiff peaks form. Gently fold the whipped cream into the cream cheese mixture until well blended and no streaks of cream remain. Spoon the filling into the cooled crust.

To garnish, sprinkle the Heath Bar pieces and pecans around the edge of the pie. Cover with plastic wrap and chill overnight in the refrigerator before serving.

MAKES ONE 9-INCH PIE

Heavenly Hash Ice Cream Pie

Heavenly Hash was one of Allysa's favorite flavors of ice cream when she was growing up. It's really difficult to find these days, so she decided to put the ingredients together in an ice cream pie and give up her supermarket search. You can use chocolate or vanilla ice cream in this recipe (or a layer of each)—both versions are great.

CRUST
½ cup (1 stick) unsalted butter, melted
2 cups chocolate wafer crumbs

MARSHMALLOW SAUCE
4 cups miniature marshmallows
⅓ cup heavy cream

FILLING
1 quart chocolate ice cream
¾ cup coarsely chopped toasted almonds (see Note)
¼ cup miniature semisweet chocolate chips

NOTE: To toast the almonds, place on a baking sheet in a 350-degree oven for 15 minutes, or until lightly browned and fragrant.

To make the crust: In a medium-size bowl, combine the butter and wafer crumbs. Press firmly into a lightly buttered 9-inch pie dish. Cover tightly with plastic wrap and place in the freezer for 1 hour.

To make the marshmallow sauce: In the top of a double boiler over barely simmering water, combine the marshmallows with the cream. Stir until the marshmallows are completely melted and the sauce is smooth, 3–5 minutes. Remove from the heat and transfer the sauce to a glass measuring cup. Allow to cool for 20 minutes.

Meanwhile, transfer the ice cream from the freezer to a covered plastic storage container and place in the refrigerator to soften for 20 minutes.

Remove the piecrust from the freezer and the ice cream from the refrigerator. Using a wooden spoon, stir the ice cream until creamy and of good spreading consistency. Spread half of the ice cream over the bottom of the prepared crust. (Allysa recommends using a small offset icing spatula if you have one.) Pour the marshmallow sauce evenly over the ice cream and sprinkle with half of the almonds. Cover tightly with plastic wrap and place in the freezer for 15 minutes to set. (Place the remaining ice cream in the freezer as well so that it doesn't get too soft.)

Remove the pie and ice cream from the freezer and carefully spread the remaining ice cream evenly over the first layer. To garnish, sprinkle the remaining almonds and the chocolate chips around the edge of the pie. Cover tightly with plastic wrap and then aluminum foil, and freeze until the pie is firm, at least 4 hours or overnight.

Let the pie soften slightly at room temperature, about 10 minutes, before slicing and serving.

MAKES ONE 9-INCH PIE

Lemon Icebox Pie

Here's a light, summery dessert for lemon lovers that's incredibly quick and easy to prepare. Just make sure you've made the Lemon Curd Filling the day before and you're all set.

CRUST
½ cup (1 stick) unsalted butter,
   very soft
2 cups vanilla wafer crumbs

FILLING
1 ½ cups heavy cream
1 ½ cups Lemon Curd Filling
   (recipe on page 139)

GARNISH (OPTIONAL)
⅓ cup fresh blueberries
Lemon slices

To make the crust: In a small bowl, combine the butter and the vanilla wafer crumbs. Press firmly into a lightly buttered 9-inch glass pie dish. Wrap tightly with plastic and place in the freezer for 30 minutes.

Meanwhile, make the filling: In a large bowl, on the medium speed of an electric mixer, beat the heavy cream until stiff peaks form. Gently fold in the Lemon Curd. Pour into the prepared crust and chill for at least 4 hours or overnight. Garnish with berries around the edge of the pie and lemon slices if desired.

MAKES ONE 9-INCH PIE

Cherry Jamboree

We started making this at the bakery when a staff member remarked that her grandmother made a dessert just like our cream cheese chocolate pudding squares but with cherry pie filling instead. It turned out to be even more popular with our customers.

CRUST
1 cup all-purpose flour
½ cup chopped toasted pecans
    (see Note)
⅓ cup (5⅓ tablespoons) unsalted
    butter, melted

CREAM CHEESE FILLING
½ pound (one 8-ounce package)
    cream cheese, softened

1 cup confectioners' sugar, sifted
1 cup heavy cream

TOPPING
One 21-ounce can cherry pie filling

GARNISH
Sweet Vanilla Whipped Cream
    (page 141)
Toasted pecan halves (see Note)

NOTE: To toast the pecans, place on a baking sheet in a 350-degree oven for 15 minutes, or until lightly browned and fragrant.

Preheat oven to 375 degrees.

To make the crust: In a small bowl, combine the flour, pecans, and butter. Press firmly into the bottom of an ungreased 8 x 8-inch glass baking dish. Bake for 15 minutes. Remove from the oven and allow to cool on a wire rack.

To make the filling: In a large bowl, on the low speed of an electric mixer, beat the cream cheese until smooth, about 2 minutes. Add the sugar and beat well. In a separate small bowl, beat the heavy cream until stiff peaks form. Gently fold the whipped cream into the cream cheese mixture.

When the crust has cooled, spread the cream cheese filling evenly over the crust using a rubber spatula. Spread the cherry pie filling on top. Cover with plastic wrap and chill for at least 2 hours or overnight. Cut into squares and serve with a dollop of whipped cream and the pecan halves.

MAKES NINE 2½-INCH SQUARES

Peanut Butter Icebox Pie

Allysa combined three of her favorite ingredients—peanut butter, caramel, and peanut butter cups—and with the help of fellow baker and peanut butter fan Ailie Alexander, came up with this treat that's a slice of heaven!

CRUST
½ cup (1 stick) unsalted butter, very soft
2 cups vanilla wafer crumbs

FILLING
12 ounces (1½ eight-ounce packages) cream cheese, softened
3 tablespoons sugar
½ teaspoon vanilla extract
¾ cup heavy cream, whipped

6 peanut butter cups, coarsely chopped (about 1 cup)
¾ cup smooth peanut butter
½ cup cold Caramel Sauce (recipe on page 140)

GARNISH
3 peanut butter cups, coarsely chopped (about ½ cup)
¼ cup finely chopped unsalted peanuts

To make the crust: In a small bowl, combine the butter and the vanilla wafer crumbs. Press firmly into a lightly buttered 9-inch glass pie dish. Wrap tightly with plastic and place in the freezer for 30 minutes.

Meanwhile, make the filling: In a large bowl, beat the cream cheese until smooth, about 2 minutes. Add the sugar gradually, continuing to beat. Add the vanilla extract. Fold in the whipped heavy cream. Then fold in the peanut butter cups.

Lightly beat the peanut butter and spoon into a pastry bag fitted with a large round tip. Set aside.

Remove crust from freezer and carefully spread the caramel in a thin layer over the bottom of the crust. Spoon half the filling on top of the caramel. Drizzle half the peanut butter over the filling, and using a small knife, swirl into the cream cheese to create a marbleized effect (if you don't have a pastry bag, drop the peanut butter by teaspoonfuls). Repeat with second half of the filling and second half of the peanut butter. Garnish with peanut butter cups and peanuts in a decorative manner.

Wrap carefully with plastic and chill overnight in the refrigerator.

MAKES ONE 9-INCH PIE

Old-fashioned Chocolate Chip Ice Cream

Allysa's been making this ice cream since she was a child and her family got their first ice cream machine. It's always been both her dad and brother's favorite flavor.

6 large egg yolks, at room temperature
⅔ cup sugar
2 cups half-and-half
1 cup heavy cream

1 tablespoon vanilla extract
1 cup miniature semisweet
    chocolate chips

In a medium-size bowl, with an eggbeater or a whisk, beat the egg yolks until creamy, 2–3 minutes. Add the sugar and beat until incorporated. Set aside.

In a double boiler over simmering water, heat the half-and-half until scalded. Add ½ cup of the half-and-half to the egg mixture, stirring to warm the egg yolks. Return the entire mixture to the double boiler and continue to cook, stirring constantly, until the mixture coats the back of a spoon, about 10 minutes. Remove from the heat and place the pot in a bowl of cold water. When the custard has cooled to room temperature, stir in the heavy cream and vanilla. Cover and refrigerate until completely chilled, preferably overnight.

Pour into an ice cream machine and freeze until partially set, about 20 minutes. Stir in the chocolate chips and continue freezing until firm, following the manufacturer's instructions.

MAKES 1 QUART

Cream Cheese
Chocolate Pudding Squares

This is another Christmastime favorite. In the midst of all of the other cooking and baking, these are simple to prepare and loved by everyone.

CRUST
2 cups flour
1 cup chopped pecans
⅔ cup (10⅔ tablespoons) unsalted
    butter, melted

CHOCOLATE PUDDING FILLING
2 packages instant chocolate
    pudding mix
3 cups whole milk

CREAM CHEESE FILLING
8 ounces (1 package) cream cheese,
    softened
1 cup sifted confectioners' sugar
1 cup heavy cream

GARNISH
Whipped cream
Pecan halves (if desired)

Preheat oven to 375 degrees.

To prepare the crust: In a small bowl, mix the flour with the pecans and the butter. Press firmly into bottom of an ungreased 13 x 9 inch baking pan. Bake for 15 minutes. Remove from oven and cool on wire rack.

Meanwhile, prepare the fillings. To prepare the chocolate pudding filling: In a large bowl, on the medium speed of an electric mixer, beat the instant pudding with the milk for 3 minutes. Place uncovered in the refrigerator and chill until set, about 15 minutes. To prepare the cream cheese filling: In a large bowl, on the low speed of an electric mixer, beat the cream cheese until smooth, about 3 minutes. Add the sugar and beat well. In a separate bowl, beat the heavy cream until stiff peaks form. Gently fold the whipped cream into the cream cheese mixture.

When crust is cooled, spread the cream cheese filling evenly over the crust, using a rubber spatula. Then spread the chocolate pudding layer on top.

Wrap and chill for at least 2 hours or overnight. Cut into squares and serve with a dollop of whipped cream. Garnish with pecan halves if desired.

MAKES TWELVE 3-INCH SQUARES

Chocolate Wafer Icebox Cake

This dessert is a variation of the traditional Nabisco chocolate wafer refrigerator log. At Allysa's house it was always made round and then sliced like a regular layer cake—probably because it was much easier for children to assemble this way.

4 cups heavy cream
3 tablespoons sugar
1 tablespoon plus 1 teaspoon
   vanilla extract

1 ½ packages (13 ½ ounces) Nabisco
   chocolate wafer cookies

In a large bowl, whip the heavy cream with the sugar and the vanilla until soft peaks form, being careful not to overwhip. To assemble the cake: On a flat plate at least 9 inches in diameter, arrange seven wafers, with one wafer in the center and the remaining six surrounding it. Scoop about ¾ cup of the whipped cream onto the wafers and gently spread the cream in a thin layer to completely cover the cookies.

Continue to layer the wafers and the cream, making sure to end with a whipped cream layer on top. Refrigerate for at least 5 hours, or overnight, before cutting and serving.

MAKES ONE 8-INCH CAKE

Magnolia's Famous Banana Pudding

Allysa started making this pudding when she was in her early twenties and cooking at a Tex-Mex restaurant and bar. Customers loved it, so when the bakery opened many years later, it seemed like a great idea to serve it there. It was the second most popular dessert (after the cupcakes) at the bakery.

One 14-ounce can sweetened
    condensed milk
1 ½ cups ice cold water
One 3.4-ounce package instant
    vanilla pudding mix (preferably
    Jell-O brand)

3 cups heavy cream
One 12-ounce box Nabisco Nilla
    Wafers (no substitutions!)
4 cups sliced ripe bananas

In a small bowl, on the medium speed of an electric mixer, beat together the sweetened condensed milk and water until well combined, about 1 minute. Add the pudding mix and beat well, about 2 minutes more. Cover and refrigerate for 3–4 hours or overnight, before continuing. It is very important to allow the proper amount of time for the pudding mixture to set.

In a large bowl, on the medium speed of an electric mixer, whip the heavy cream until stiff peaks form. Gently fold the pudding mixture into the whipped cream until well blended and no streaks of pudding remain.

To assemble the dessert, select a large, wide bowl (preferably glass) with a 4–5-quart capacity. Arrange one-third of the wafers to cover the bottom of the bowl, overlapping if necessary, then one-third of the bananas and one-third of the pudding. Repeat the layering twice more, garnishing with additional wafers or wafer crumbs on the top layer of the pudding. Cover tightly with plastic wrap and allow to chill in the refrigerator for 4 hours—or up to 8 hours, but no longer!—before serving.

SERVES 12–15

Vanilla Sandwich Creme Cookie Ice Cream

For vanilla lovers, this is like the well-known "cookies and cream" or "Oreo" ice creams, but it is made with vanilla cookies instead of chocolate.

6 large egg yolks, at room temperature
⅔ cup sugar
2 cups half-and-half
1 cup heavy cream

1 tablespoon vanilla extract
12 vanilla sandwich cookies (such as Nabisco or Famous Amos), broken into quarters

In a medium-size bowl, with an eggbeater or a whisk, beat the egg yolks until creamy, 2–3 minutes. Add the sugar and beat until incorporated. Set aside.

In a double boiler over simmering water, heat the half-and-half until scalded. Add ½ cup of the half-and-half to the egg mixture, stirring to warm the egg yolks. Return the entire mixture to the double boiler and continue to cook, stirring constantly, until the mixture coats the back of a spoon, about 10 minutes. Remove from the heat and place the pot in a bowl of cold water. When the custard has cooled to room temperature, stir in the cream and vanilla. Cover and refrigerate until completely chilled, preferably overnight.

Pour into an ice cream machine and freeze until partially set, about 20 minutes. Stir in the broken cookie pieces and continue freezing until firm, following the manufacturer's instructions.

MAKES 1 QUART

Chocolate Pudding Trifle

Here's an easy dessert that was the result of an "accident" at the bakery one day. Some small chocolate cakes refused to come out of their pans (someone forgot to grease and flour!). Sad at the thought of throwing out all that delicious cake, Jennifer assembled layers of broken cake, pudding, whipped cream, and chocolate cookie crumbs. The results were fabulous, and many customers come back asking if any more "mistakes" have been made so they can have their terrific trifle!

CHOCOLATE CAKE

Use your favorite chocolate cake recipe or even a box of your favorite chocolate cake mix. Allow cake to cool for 15 minutes before proceeding. Break up the cake into small pieces in a large bowl.

CHOCOLATE PUDDING FILLING

2 packages instant chocolate pudding mix
3 cups whole milk

WHIPPED CREAM

2 cups heavy cream
1 ½ tablespoons sugar
2 teaspoons vanilla extract

GARNISH

About 1 cup chocolate wafer crumbs, or chocolate-sandwich cookies, crushed into crumbs

Prepare the chocolate cake as recommended above.

To prepare the chocolate pudding filling: In a large bowl, on the medium speed of an electric mixer, beat the instant pudding and the milk for 3 minutes. Place uncovered in the refrigerator and chill until set, about 15 minutes.

Meanwhile, in a medium-size bowl, whip the heavy cream with the sugar and the vanilla extract until soft peaks form, being careful not to overwhip.

To assemble the trifle: Place ⅓ of the cake in the bottom of a large glass bowl. Place over this ⅓ of the pudding mixture, spreading evenly with a rubber spatula. Spread ⅓ of the whipped cream over this. Sprinkle with ⅓ of the cookie crumbs. Proceed in this fashion until three layers have been assembled, ending with a dusting of the cookie crumbs. Refrigerate at least 2 hours, or overnight, before cutting and serving.

FILLS A 6-QUART BOWL ABOUT ¾ OF THE WAY

Lemon Pudding with Raspberries and Gingersnaps

Former Magnolia manager Margaret Hathaway came up with this delightful spring-time dessert that is based on the banana pudding.

8 large egg yolks, at room temperature
2 cups sugar
½ cup cornstarch
3 cups warm water
½ cup (1 stick) unsalted butter, melted
    and cooled to room temperature

1½ cups fresh lemon juice
1 teaspoon grated lemon zest
3 cups heavy cream
12 ounces gingersnap cookies
    (any popular boxed brand is fine)
1 pint fresh raspberries

In a medium-size bowl, with an eggbeater or a whisk, beat the egg yolks until creamy, 2–3 minutes. Set aside.

In a large saucepan, combine the sugar and cornstarch. Gradually add the water and cook over medium heat, stirring constantly, until the mixture thickens, about 5 minutes.

Remove from the heat and add 2 cups of the hot mixture to the egg yolks, stirring to warm the egg yolks. Return the entire mixture to the pot and heat 1 minute more.

Remove from the heat and stir in the butter, lemon juice, and lemon zest. Transfer to a medium-size bowl and cool to room temperature, about 1 hour.

In a large bowl, on the medium speed of an electric mixer, whip the cream until stiff peaks form. Gently fold the pudding mixture into the whipped cream until well blended and no streaks of pudding remain.

To assemble the dessert, select a large, wide bowl (preferably glass) with a 4–5-quart capacity. Arrange one-third of the gingersnaps to cover the bottom of the bowl, overlapping if necessary, then one-third of the pudding. Repeat the layering twice more. Garnish the top layer with raspberries. Cover tightly with plastic wrap and allow to chill in the refrigerator for 4 hours—or up to 8 hours, but no longer!—before serving.

SERVES 12–15

Metric Equivalencies

LIQUID AND DRY MEASURE EQUIVALENCIES

CUSTOMARY	METRIC
¼ teaspoon	1.25 milliliters
½ teaspoon	2.5 milliliters
1 teaspoon	5 milliliters
1 tablespoon	15 milliliters
1 fluid ounce	30 milliliters
¼ cup	60 milliliters
⅓ cup	80 milliliters
½ cup	120 milliliters
1 cup	240 milliliters
1 pint (*2 cups*)	480 milliliters
1 quart (*4 cups, 32 ounces*)	960 milliliters (*.96 liter*)
1 gallon (*4 quarts*)	3.84 liters
1 ounce (*by weight*)	28 grams
¼ pound (*4 ounces*)	114 grams
1 pound (*16 ounces*)	454 grams
2.2 pounds	1 kilogram (*1,000 grams*)

OVEN-TEMPERATURE EQUIVALENCIES

DESCRIPTION	°FAHRENHEIT	°CELSIUS
Cool	200	90
Very slow	250	120
Slow	300–325	150–160
Moderately slow	325–350	160–180
Moderate	350–375	180–190
Moderately hot	375–400	190–200
Hot	400–450	200–230
Very hot	450–500	230–260

Index